SHOP LIKE A
CHEF

A FOOD LOVER'S GUIDE
TO ST. LOUIS NEIGHBORHOODS

by Chef Clara Moore
and Matt Sorrell

FIRST EDITION

EVERYTHING GOES MEDIA
WWW.EVERYTHINGGOESMEDIA.COM
CHICAGO & MILWAUKEE

ST. LUCIUS FIRELIGHTS
WWW.SHOPLIKEACHEF.COM
ST. LOUIS

Shop Like a Chef:
A Food Lover's Guide to St. Louis Neighborhoods
by Chef Clara Moore and Matt Sorrell

Published November 2013 by:

Everything Goes Media, LLC
www.everything goes.com
with
St. Lucius Firelights
www.ShopLikeaChef.com

Publisher's Cataloging-In-Publication Data
(Prepared by The Donohue Group, Inc.)

Moore, Clara, 1981-
   Shop like a chef : a food lover's guide to St. Louis neighborhoods / Clara
Moore and Matt Sorrell. -- 1st ed.

   p. : ill. ; cm.

   Includes index.
   ISBN: 978-1-893121-95-9

   1. Grocery shopping--Missouri--Saint Louis--Guidebooks. 2. Farmers' markets-
-Missouri--Saint Louis--Guidebooks. 3. Ethnic markets--Missouri--Saint Louis--
Guidebooks. 4. St. Louis (Mo.)--Guidebooks. I. Sorrell, Matt. II. Title.

TX356 .M66 2013
381/.41/02577866   2013939511

18 17 16 15 14 13   10 9 8 7 6 5 4 3 2 1

Really, at the end of the day, this is for my mother. The years of dragging me to the grocery store and imparting her love of words made this book possible.
— C.M.

To my wife, Beth, for her unwavering support for all of my creative endeavors.
— M.S.

MAP OF ST. LOUIS

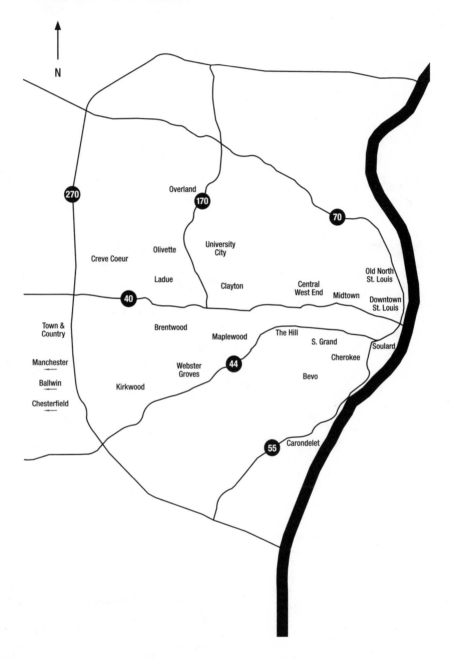

CONTENTS

FOREWORD

I love grocery shopping. I always have. Even when I was a young girl growing up in a small Midwestern town in the '80s, I adored Saturday mornings at the IGA. The automatic doors would swoosh open and I would rush directly to the produce section. My mother would assign me certain items from her grocery list, and I would take off on my scavenger hunt. I marveled at the beautiful fruits and vegetables in the bins. I gently stroked the fuzzy skins of kiwis. I breathed in the sweet aroma of plump strawberries. I shook the heads of freshly washed romaine and watched the water droplets rain down around me. I even popped a few crisp, juicy grapes into my mouth after making sure I was out of sight of the manager. Minutes later I would return to my mother with my arms full of onions, carrots, potatoes, apples, and more. Then I would hitch a ride on the cart, like a tourist on a cable car, as she slowly made her way through every aisle in the store. When the spirit moved me, I would sneak a box of cookies or popsicles into the cart, but they were always vetoed at the checkout lane when my mom loaded our goods onto the conveyor belt. (Okay, sometimes she let a box of Fudgsicles through. She is a great mom—and a fan of Fudgsicles.)

Not much has changed in the last twenty-five years when it comes to me and grocery shopping. Now I live in St. Louis, and I hit the town enthusiastically every Saturday morning with my grocery list. Shopping is an adventure for me. One that starts with a great cup of locally roasted coffee and some fresh baked pastries for the trip. Because this is going to take half the day. I can't be satisfied with going to just one store. I have a passion for cooking and with that comes a passion for ingredients. If pizza is on the menu, I have to visit The Hill for "00" flour and housemade pepperoni. When tomato season arrives, I follow up my farmers market visit with a trip to the Cherokee Street *tiendas* for freshly made tortillas, chorizo, and *cotija* cheese to accompany the many salsas I'll make when I get home. And, when I'm planning a party, I head first to myriad specialty shops for the best selection of cheeses, meats, and housemade condiments to serve my guests.

Over the years of Saturday morning excursions, I've come to know many shop owners in St. Louis. We're kindred spirits we folk who derive pleasure from discovering exceptional ingredients and well-made products. These owners know me by name, know what I like to buy, and know which new items to turn me on to. They are masters of their domains. Their knowledge and passion are what make grocery shopping fun. And that is an experience most people don't associate with shopping. This is what makes Clara and Matt's book so very important. Most people I know say they hate grocery shopping. And I believe that's because it's impersonal for them. It's a chore that, like vacuuming or laundry, is just another item on their weekend to-do list that does nothing more than get in the way of their free time.

The joy of grocery shopping is a lost art. One that has fallen victim to bulk buying and value hunting. Instead, it should be an enjoyable journey that involves learning more about food, where it comes from, and the people who are selling it. St. Louis is a treasure trove of culinary delights, not only in our restaurants but in the many shops devoted to quality goods. With *Shop Like A Chef: A Food Lover's Guide To St. Louis Neighborhoods*, Clara and Matt have made it easy to fall in love with grocery shopping all over again (or, in some cases, for the first time). Whether you live in St. Louis or are here as our guest, this guide to notable local food shops will help you discover a whole new world of ingredients and food stuffs—be they exotic, gourmet, or simply fresh and delicious—throughout the area. Just be sure when you're exploring these stores to take the time to stroke some kiwis or shake some lettuce. It does wonders for your soul.

—Brandi Wills

Managing Editor, *Feast Magazine*

INTRODUCTION

By Chef Clara Moore

This project was brought to me a number of years ago by publisher Sharon Woodhouse at Lake Claremont Press. Their two editions of *A Cook's Guide to Chicago* were a big hit and she was looking to expand the idea to St. Louis. I worked on the local version for two years—first while I was trying to figure out what direction I was taking my career and then during the first year I worked as executive chef at Local Harvest Café. But the project subsequently died. The economy crashed, the café got popular, life happened. I cringed anytime someone asked, "How is the book going?" "Nowhere!" I thought, but I usually only smiled with a response like, "Oh, you know…"

This book was originally written to be a direct St. Louis counterpart of *A Cook's Guide to Chicago* and reflected that in content and layout. But after setting the manuscript down for a few years and returning to it with fresh eyes, I found that I wanted to speak more from my heart and experience. It morphed more into a "Cook and Eat Local, Seasonal, Small, and Independent Guide to St. Louis" or "The Joy of Shopping Through a Chef's Eyes"!

When I was initially approached about writing this book, my reaction was, "Of course, I want nothing more than to help people expand their cooking endeavors, and I already know most of the places I can write about."

The first part of that reaction remains true. Author Marilyn Pocius says about the original *Cook's Guide*: "[It] began as a simple idea: Tell home cooks where to go to get the ingredients and equipment they need or want." Much like her book, I expand on that basic premise and seek to wow readers with the beautiful bounty of food in my hometown, and to make "exotic" ingredients much more accessible.

The second half of my thinking—that I was already acquainted with most of the places that would end up in this book—couldn't have been further from the truth. Throughout the writing process, I have found so many hidden treasures and tiny gems buried in strip malls and on the less-traveled roads of the St. Louis metro area. Over and over again I have been surprised by just what is available in this city, and the overwhelming diversity of ingredients. And I didn't even cover what can be found in any of the big local or national grocery chains, though many now have dedicated aisles for ethnic and gourmet ingredients.

My goal for this book is to inform and inspire. I hope to nudge you outside of your normal food gathering habits to explore the rich market culture of St. Louis—to make grocery shopping exciting again, to make hard-to-find ingredients easier to find, and to get you and others into the kitchen and cooking!

DISCLAIMER

Shop Like a Chef is by no means a thorough reference book of the cultures or neighborhoods of greater St. Louis. Cuisines, as well as neighborhoods, are incredibly complicated and very regional. My co-author Matt Sorrell and I have tried to touch on important facts, food, or flavors of these categories and their effect on St. Louis. Cities are in flux and constantly changing—small businesses open and close with amazing frequency. We have tried to offer a good cross-section of cultures and stores in the metro area, and I hope we have not yet discovered every worthy little grocery in the city. [On that note, feel free to contact me with any of your favorites we overlooked for the next edition!]

The opinions expressed are ours—purely and without a doubt personal—and they are just opinions at that. We visited many stores only once or twice, so the experience or products are subject to change.

HOW TO USE THIS BOOK

Shop Like a Chef is a guide to help navigate the complicated, and sometimes confusing, world of small grocery stores. We begin with a chapter on neighborhoods, which includes a short explanation of the predominant style and basic ethnic makeup of each community. Included in each of these sections is a list of the diverse and interesting stores located there. Stores and markets that naturally fit into more than one category are listed in every applicable chapter, with a reference to the page than contains the full description.

The rest of the chapters are organized by type or cuisine of the stores. Each chapter begins with a general description of the type of stores or cuisine examined, followed by a list of common and useful items sold at these types of stores with brief descriptions. Then come entries devoted to the stores, recipes, and hints.

Remember what I said about nudging you? We added checkboxes next to each establishment so that you can keep track of where you've been and what grocery exploits still await. Space for notes has been added at all the strategic spots so that you can truly make it your own and continue enhancing your St. Louis food and cooking experiences. Throughout the book we've left some extra space, so even where we haven't given you lines, I encourage you to fill that up with your customizations and build for yourself your own culinary field guide or scrapbook.

Finally, we've given this book one heck of an index so that you can turn to it again and again to find just what you're looking for. Keep a copy of this book wherever you're most likely to need it...in the kitchen, in the glove box, or at the front door, ready for your next adventure.

NEIGHBORHOODS

St. Louis neighborhoods have seen a lot of change over the last seventy-five years, not the least of which has been population shifts with significant social, cultural, and financial consequences for many of them. In 1950, the population of the city of St. Louis was just under 857,000, while St. Louis County was at roughly 406,000. St. Charles County just to the west had only a population of 30,000 or so, about the same size as some of the smaller municipalities in St. Louis County. As of the latest census, the city had declined in population to 319,000, while the county was hovering at just under 1,000,000. The population exodus continued even further westward— St. Charles County has ballooned to 360,000, and is now more populous than St. Louis itself.

This decline in population in the city has changed the landscape of each borough, many struggling to keep what used to be their thriving economy afloat. This seems to be a theme that runs through most of the neighborhood descriptions in this chapter, though it needs to be said that these places are full of people working very hard to retain their community, culture, and the interesting diversity these conditions have created. You'll see another recurring theme: rejuvenation, new creative energy, and passionate small businesses.

There are a lot of ideas and opinions out there as to what constitutes a true and proper St. Louis neighborhood. Some say it has to have definite boundaries and organization, an official name, and validated perhaps by the existence of a newsletter and regularly scheduled resident meetings. Others believe that to be considered a neighborhood an area must have a specific ethnic or cultural identity. And on and on. Some of the "neighborhoods" we've written about fit into such specific parameters, some don't. A good portion are actually complete municipalities unto themselves, while others are just a loose collection of blocks that have developed over time into cohesive entities with their own specific personalities. What they all have in common is the existence of a wide variety of vibrant and vital culinary purveyors, and more depth and history than many of us realize.

The little write-ups below aren't definitive histories or analyses. Far from it. Our hope is that this collection of brief sketches will provide you enough insight into how these areas arrived where they are today and spark your interest in exploring them further, starting with the distinctive markets, stores, shops, and emporiums that call them home.

SOUTH CITY

South City is a large and diverse set of neighborhoods, four of which are outlined in this section, below is a list of great stores that don't fall into those distinct areas. Enjoy your exploration!

☐ CARONDELET FARMERS' MARKET
carondeletfarmersmarket.wordpress.com
7701 S. Broadway
Carondelet
Saturdays, June–October
7 a.m.–Noon
See entry on p. 100.

☐ G&W
4828 Parker Ave.
South City
314/352-5066
See entry on p. 127.

☐ LE GRAND'S MARKET & CATERING
legrandsmarket-catering.com
4414 Donovan Ave.
St. Louis Hills
314/353-6128
See entry on p. 128.

☐ LOCAL HARVEST GROCERY
localharvestgrocery.com
3148 Morganford Rd.
Tower Grove South
314/865-5260
See entry on p. 82.

☐ MAUDE'S MARKET
maudesmarket.com
4219 Virginia Ave.
South City
314/353-4219
See entry on p. 83.

☐ RANDALL'S
shoprandalls.com
1910 S. Jefferson Ave.
South City
314/865-0199
See entry on p. 144.

☐ TOWER GROVE FARMERS' MARKET
tgmarket.org
Tower Grove Park,
near the Pool Pavilion
South City Saturdays, May–October
8 a.m.–Noon
See entry on p. 104.

NOTES ON SOUTH CITY

_____

_____

_____

_____

_____

_____

_____

_____

_____

_____

_____

DINE AROUND
PARTICIPANT

SOUTH GRAND

Not exactly a neighborhood but rather a social and commercial thoroughfare, this vibrant, bustling strip of South Grand Boulevard stretches from around Arsenal Street at the edge of historic Tower Grove Park to Chippewa Street, providing the western border of the Compton Heights and Tower Grove East neighborhoods. All manner of ethnic eateries are packed within this handful of blocks, from Thai to Vietnamese to Ethiopian, as well as bars, specialty boutiques, and mom-and-pop shops of all descriptions, including a host of LGBT-friendly businesses. It's also home to Jays International Market, one of the most popular multicultural groceries in the metro area.

The area is eminently walkable, and strolling down its sidewalks makes one part of a pageant of sights and sounds. Folks in the traditional dress of their native lands mix with an assortment of inked-up hipsters, college students, foodies, travelers, artists, and sundry bohemian types.

The languages of a dozen countries can be heard wafting out of open doors and windows. Despite the preponderance of ethnic stores and eateries on South Grand, the residential breakdown of the area is roughly half black and half white, with statistically few Latinos or Asians claiming residence here.

History buffs also have plenty to experience in the vicinity, like the Compton Heights Water Tower and Park, just a bit north on Grand near I-44. The iconic tower was erected in 1898 to camouflage a 100-foot-tall standpipe that was built to equalize local water pressure. The Magic Chef Mansion, located a couple of blocks east of Grand on Russell Avenue, was built in 1908 for Charles Stockstrom, founder of what would eventually become the Magic Chef Stove Company, and is available for tours.

☐ AFGHAN MARKET
3740 S. Grand Blvd.
South City
314/664-5555
See entry on p. 176.

☐ BAGHDAD MARKET
3730 S. Grand Blvd.
South City
See entry on p. 177.

☐ INTERNATIONAL FOODS
3905 S. Grand Blvd.
South City
314/351-9495
See entry on p. 214.

☐ JAY'S INTERNATIONAL
3172 S. Grand Blvd.
South City
314/772-2552
See entry on p. 221.

☐ NEW DAWN NATURAL FOODS
3536 Arsenal St.
South City
314/772-9110
See entry on p. 72.

☐ THE VINE
3171 S. Grand Blvd.
South City
314/776-0991
See entry on p. 178.

NOTES ON SOUTH GRAND

_____

_____

_____

_____

_____

_____

_____

_____

_____

_____

_____

CHEROKEE

The Cherokee Street business district sprang up in the late 1800s and quickly became a bustling commercial hub, thanks in large part to the electric streetcar tracks that were installed there in the later part of the century. By 1912, the stretch of Cherokee Street from Oregon Avenue to Jefferson Avenue was overflowing with activity, home to multiple dry goods stores, saloons, groceries, barbershops, druggists, and the like. As many as three separate dental practices simultaneously called the neighborhood home at one point. The area continued to flourish until the 1960s, when urban blight and the slow exodus of city residents to the suburbs began to chip away at the once thriving neighborhood.

But Cherokee experienced a resurgence starting in the 1980s. That decade brought an influx of Latinos relocating to St. Louis, with many of them opening businesses—mainly grocery stores and bakeries—in and around Cherokee. Real estate in the vicinity was cheap, and it was close to many Catholic churches, such as St. Pius, St. Francis de Sales, St. Anthony of Padua, and St. Cecilia's. Families would attend mass on Sundays, then head down to Cherokee to shop. One of the first such businesses to open during this era was the Rio Grande Grocery Store, which stood for close to 30 years. While Cherokee has benefitted tremendously from the Hispanic community's commercial activity, few Latinos reside in the area. According to the 2010 census, just nine percent of Cherokee area residents are Latino.

Though the economic situation has become markedly better for the Cherokee neighborhood in recent history, the area is still littered with abandoned buildings and neglected properties. Over the last decade or so, Cherokee Street has become home to a small but active enclave of artists, activists, and entrepreneurs who are reclaiming many of these neglected storefronts and shuttered edifices and repurposing them. Currently there are art galleries and studios, letter presses like Firecracker Press (2838 Cherokee St.), restaurants and bars, theaters, and a plethora of other endeavors co-existing with long-standing businesses, and together creating a dynamic and growing cultural and commercial scene. While Cherokee Street still has a long way to go, it seems to be slowly finding its way back to its glory days of the last century. Only time will tell.

☐ **CARNICERÍA LATINO AMERICANA**
2800 Cherokee St.
South City

5412 S. Grand Blvd.
South City
314/481-3665
See entry on p. 155.

☐ **EL TORITO**
2753 Cherokee St.
South City
314/771-8648
See entry on p. 159.

NOTES ON CHEROKEE

_____

_____

_____

_____

_____

_____

_____

_____

_____

_____

BEVO

Bounded by Chippewa Street to the north, Holly Hills Avenue to the south, South Kingshighway Boulevard on the west side, and Gustine Terrace to the east, the Bevo neighborhood was originally settled by some of the city's many German immigrants. This Teutonic heritage is still evident all across the area, from streets with names like *Eichelberger* and *Schirmer* to architectural features like the flat-front brick row houses and the commercial buildings with facades resembling Alpine lodges. The Bevo neighborhood is built on a landscape of steep hills and crisscrossed by streets that intersect at crazy angles and veer off in unexpected directions, giving even the most seasoned local reason to consult a GPS.

The neighborhood takes its name from the Bevo Mill that sits like a sentinel in the center of the neighborhood at the intersection of Gravois Avenue and Morgan Ford Road. This beloved landmark was built by August A. Busch, Sr., son of Anheuser-Busch founder Adolphus Busch—one of the most famous of St. Louis's German immigrants—in 1916 for a then-staggering $250,000. A replica of a European windmill, the building was open to the public as a restaurant from 1917 until 2009, when it became primarily a private event space.

Bevo has seen the arrival of a sizeable number of Bosnian immigrants over the last twenty years. This has helped revitalize the neighborhood's economy, which had suffered since after World War II as residents moved west to the ever-expanding suburbs. Many Bosnian shops, markets, and eateries dot the area, places like the emblematic Grbic Restaurant & Banquet Center at 4071 Keokuk Street. Amidst this renewed economic vigor, decaying reminders of Bevo's previous commercial prosperity still abound. Check out the crumbling Art Deco National Candy Company factory at 4230 Gravois Avenue, and what's left of the Alligator Oil Clothing Company buildings on Bingham Avenue.

☐ EUROPA MARKET
5005 Gravois Ave.
Bevo
314/481-9880
See entry on p. 167.

☐ IRISKIC BROTHERS MESNICA BUTCHER
5411 Gravois Rd.
Bevo
314/752-3488
See entry on p. 168.

☐ SOUTH CITY MEAT (MESNICA)
5201 Gravois Ave.
Bevo
314/457-8107
See entry on p. 169.

☐ ZLANTO ZITO
4573 Gravois Ave.
Bevo
314/752-3004
See entry on p. 170.

NOTES ON BEVO

_____
_____
_____
_____
_____
_____
_____
_____
_____
_____
_____

THE HILL

Despite its reputation as St. Louis's premier Italian enclave, The Hill was originally settled by English Quakers, as well as the German and Irish immigrants who moved there in the 1830s to mine a recently discovered clay deposit. Italians, primarily Sicilians, began to immigrate to St. Louis and settle in the area in the 1890s; it was their culture that took root and gave the area its identity. The boundaries of The Hill are Kingshighway Boulevard, Hampton Avenue, Columbia Avenue, and Southwest Avenue. A large portion of the neighborhood's current population still claims Italian descent.

One of the most striking aspects of The Hill—so named because of its relatively high elevation—is the overall cleanliness and tidiness of its streets, homes, and businesses. The Hill's many narrow roads lined with rows of neat bungalows fronted by well-trimmed lawns, many flying the familiar green, orange, and white

Italian flag from their porches are indeed one of our town's most stirring and comforting sights.

The mines and most industrial concerns are long gone now, and the neighborhood is primarily known for its small businesses, many still family-owned. Of particular note are the Italian restaurants and markets that permeate the area. Diners can choose from a variety of culinary experiences on The Hill, whether casual or formal, regional Italian or Italian American. Home cooks who head there to shop invariably come away with a bounty of Italian delicacies, from cured meats and imported cheeses to fresh breads and pastas.

If there's one edifice that defines The Hill, it's St. Ambrose Roman Catholic Church at 5130 Wilson Avenue. This church was first built in 1903, then rebuilt in the 1920s after being destroyed by fire. For over a century it's been the spiritual, cultural, and architectural epicenter of the neighborhood.

☐ **BERTARELLI CUTLERY**
bertarellicutlery.com
1927 Marconi Ave.
The Hill
314/664-4005
See entry on p. 45.

☐ **DIGREGORIO'S ITALIAN FOODS**
5200 Daggett Ave.
The Hill
314/776-1062
See entry on p. 184.

☐ **URZI'S ITALIAN MARKET**
5430 Southwest Ave.
The Hill
314/645-3914
See entry on p. 185.

☐ **VIVIANO AND SONS GROCERS**
shopviviano.com
5139 Shaw Ave.
The Hill
314/771-5524
See entry on p. 186.

☐ **VOLPI ITALIAN SALAMI & MEAT COMPANY**
volpifoods.com
5263 Northrup Ave.
The Hill
314/772-8550
See entry on p. 60.

NOTES ON THE HILL

_____

_____

_____

_____

_____

_____

_____

_____

_____

_____

_____

MIDTOWN AND THE CENTRAL WEST END

Midtown, referred to as such because it's basically the geographic center of the city of St. Louis, is bounded by Delmar Boulevard to the north, Chouteau Avenue, on the south side, 21st Street to the east, and Vandeventer Avenue on the west. The area was mostly rural until the mid-1800s when it experienced rapid growth and expansion thanks to new residents like Saint Louis University, which set up shop there in 1888 and quickly became a focal point for development. Midtown is still heavily influenced by the will and whims of this institution.

Midtown really took off as both a commercial as well as a cultural center in the early 1900s with the addition of electrified streetcars. The proliferation of dance halls, ballrooms, theaters, hotels, saloons, and restaurants soon followed. Several hospitals operated in the vicinity during this period, and many of the physicians associated with them occupied office space in Midtown. From the 1920s through WWII, Midtown was also home to Automobile Row, a couple of blocks on Locust Street where a bevy of auto dealers hawked their wares. It was the place to buy a horseless carriage in St. Louis. Officially referred to as the Locust Street Automotive District, it was added to the National Register of Historic Places in 2005.

The area has seen important revitalization in recent years, starting perhaps most famously with the rehab of the Fabulous Fox Theatre in the mid-1990s. That success story spurred the undertaking of other significant residential and commercial projects as developers have sought to breathe new life into classic works of famous architects or match them with new edifices. One of these notable architects is Preston Bradshaw, designer of such historic buildings as the Autocar Sales and Service Building at 2745 Locust on Automobile Row and the Chase Park Plaza Hotel a bit west in Central West End.

Today Midtown is reliving some of its past glory. Once again it is home to an entertainment district that features The Fox Theatre as well as the Sheldon Concert Hall, the Grandel Theater, and Powell Symphony Hall among other venues. A slew of popular restaurants has also taken up residence in Midtown, including The Fountain On Locust, Pappy's Smokehouse, and the St. Louis location of Hamburger Mary's.

In the later part of the 1800s, many of St. Louis's wealthy denizens were seeking to distance themselves from the increasingly crowded conditions (and lower class residents) that were prevailing in the city. Many of the elite began migrating to what at the time was the western limit of the city near the large Forest Park, where there was plenty of prime real estate available to erect the mansions and monuments that would come to define the area. What became known as the Central West End has been home to many of the city's famous literary denizens, including Kate Chopin, Tennessee Williams, and T.S. Eliot. It also boasts some of St. Louis's most impressive structures, namely the awe-inspiring Cathedral Basilica (4431 N. Lindell Blvd.) and the stately Art Deco Chase Park Plaza (212 N. Kingshighway).

Like many areas of the city, the post-WWII years saw a general decline in the CWE, both in terms of population and in the condition of many of the properties there, though a number of its exclusive private drives like Westmoreland Place, Portland Place, Kingsbury Place, and Hortense Place retained a modicum of dignity and stately grace. Some of the blight still exists, particularly on the northern edge of the enclave, but many of the historic homes and commercial buildings have been preserved, restored, and otherwise revitalized.

While the CWE was originally settled by white Europeans and their immediate descendants, the area now claims sizable African-American and Asian populations. Large transient student and professional populations—thanks to the proximity of the Barnes-Jewish Hospital and Medical Center and the campuses of Washington University that border both sides of Forest Park—add to the neighborhood's distinctive flavor. That the area is currently home to some of the city's best restaurants and nightspots is not surprising, but keep

an eye out for other attractions like the World Chess Hall of Fame (4652 Maryland Ave.) too!

☐ **GOLDEN GROCER NATURAL FOODS**
goldengrocer.com
335 N. Euclid Ave.
Central West End
314/367-0405
See entry on p. 70.

☐ **STRAUB'S**
straubs.com
302 N. Kingshighway Blvd.
Central West End
314/361-6646
See entry on p. 58.

NOTES ON MIDTOWN AND THE CENTRAL WEST END

_____

_____

_____

_____

_____

_____

_____

_____

_____

_____

NORTH SIDE

The term *North Side* is much used and misused by St. Louisans. It's more often than not a blanket term meant to cover a plethora of areas in the northern realm of the city and county alike.

On the city side, North Side can refer to a multitude of neighborhoods, including College Hill, Walnut Park, Riverview, and the aptly named Old North St. Louis, which was established in 1816 as the Village of North St. Louis and annexed by the city in 1941. This northern region was settled by the whole gamut of European immigrants that came to St. Louis, Germans, English, and Irish most prevalent among them. Some of the city's richest architectural and historical sites are located up north, including Bellefontaine and Calvary Cemeteries in North Riverfront. The area suffered massive decay and population loss in the years after World War II. There are countless heart-breaking examples of some of the finest private and commercial architecture that ever graced the cityscape now standing in ruins, fit only to be razed. But there is hope for the North Side. New businesses are starting to crop up, and the population in some neighborhoods is on the rebound. In the 2010 census, for example, Old North St. Louis showed a population increase of almost twenty-eight percent since 2000.

The sprawl of North St. Louis County is made up of a variety of municipalities, including Ferguson, Florissant, Berkeley, Jennings, Normandy, and Pine Lawn, and a gaggle of smaller neighborhoods. This area of the county is home to the first ring of St. Louis suburbs that rose up as the urban population began to flow west, although some of the first communities there, like Bellefontaine Neighbors and Grande Prairie, were settled as far back as the late 1700s and early 1800s by German and French settlers. Some, like Black Jack, Ferguson, and Florissant a bit further west, began as farming communities. Like its sister area inside the city limits, North County has seen some hard times, but the future looks promising.

☐ **DAYLIGHT NUTRITION**
8565 Airport Rd.
Berkeley
314/522-8804
See entry on p. 69.

☐ **FERGUSON FARMERS MARKET**
fergusonfarmersmarket.com
20 S. Florissant Rd.
Ferguson
314/524-1820
Saturdays, April–November, 8 a.m.–Noon
See entry on p. 101.

☐ **FORD HOTEL AND RESTAURANT SUPPLY**
fordstl.com
2204 N. Broadway
North Downtown
314/231-8400 or 800/472-3673
See entry on p. 46.

☐ **MEAT FAIR**
2315 Chambers Rd.
North County
314/868-9118
See entry on p. 129.

☐ **NORTH CITY FARMERS' MARKET**
northcityfarmersmarket.blogspot.com
St. Louis Ave. and N. 14th St., in front of Crown Candy Kitchen
Saturdays, June–October, 9 a.m.–Noon
See entry on p. 102.

☐ **PAUL'S MARKET**
paulsmarketdeli.com
1020 N. Elizabeth Ave.
Ferguson
314/524-3652
See entry on p. 130.

□ PICCOLINO'S ITALIAN GROCER
piccolinosfoodandwine.com
10 Church St.
Ferguson
314/942-2255
See entry on p. 185.

□ PIEKUTOWSKI'S EUROPEAN STYLE
piekutowskimeat.webs.com
4100 N. Florissant Ave.
North City
314/534-6256
See entry on p. 131.

□ RANDALL'S
shoprandalls.com
11000 Old Halls Ferry Rd.
North County
314/741-5100
See entry on p. 144.

NOTES ON THE NORTH SIDE

_____

_____

_____

_____

_____

_____

_____

_____

_____

_____

CLAYTON

The city of Clayton was named after Ralph Clayton, a local who offered up some free land to establish a county seat in 1877, just a year after the big St. Louis city/county split, and the city is still the center of St. Louis County government today. Height requirements for new buildings were ditched in 1957, paving the way for the high-rise buildings that make up the current downtown Clayton skyline. During the lunch hour, workers empty out of these towers of commerce and crowd onto the sidewalks to take advantage of the many dining options available. After the workday, downtown Clayton comes alive as diners stream in to enjoy the trendy eateries that abound here.

While Clayton is well known as a commercial and governmental hub, it's not all about glass and steel. Hanley House, an 1850s farmhouse-turned-museum and one of the only vestiges of the city's rural past, still stands virtually untouched by time at 7600 Westmoreland. The Seven Gables building at 26 N. Meramec Avenue, built in 1926 as a combo residential/commercial development, is a refreshing little Tudor Revival oasis amid the expanse of concrete and metal. It now houses the boutique hotel Seven Gables Inn. Some eighty-one percent of Clayton real estate is either residential or park land, so there's plenty of green space

to be had. One favorite is Shaw Park, home to the city's aquatic center and skating rink, among other amenities, and host to a variety of outdoor events. From May through November, the Clayton Farmer's Market brings some of the best local purveyors to the city to sell their wares at 8282 Forsyth Blvd., just west of Straub's.

☐ **CLAYTON FARMER'S MARKET**
claytonfarmersmarket.com
8282 Forsyth Blvd.
Clayton
Saturdays, late May–late October
8:30 a.m. –12:30 p.m.
See entry on p. 100.

☐ **KITCHEN CONSERVATORY**
kitchenconservatory.com
8021 Clayton Rd.
Clayton
314/862-2665 or 886/862-2433
See entry on p. 47.

☐ **PARKER'S TABLE**
parkerstable.com
7118 Oakland Ave.
Clayton
314/645-2050
See entry on p. 56.

☐ **STRAUB'S**
straubs.com
8282 Forsyth Blvd.
Clayton
314/725-2121
See entry on p. 58.

☐ THE WINE AND CHEESE PLACE
wineandcheeseplace.com
7435 Forsyth Blvd.
Clayton
314/727-8788
See entry on p. 146.

☐ THE WINE MERCHANT
winemerchantltd.com
20 S. Hanley Rd.
Clayton
314/863-6282
See entry on p. 147.

NOTES ON CLAYTON

_____
_____
_____
_____
_____
_____
_____
_____
_____
_____

MAPLEWOOD, BRENTWOOD, AND WEBSTER

The cities of Maplewood, Brentwood, and Webster are clustered together just to the west of the city of St. Louis. Maplewood is the closest to the city, right inside the county line. It was part of the original land grant given to Charles Gratiot by the Spanish government in 1798, and was incorporated in 1908. Maplewood began as a mostly residential area but soon developed a commercial side as well, gaining importance early on because of the street car turnaround loop located on Sutton Avenue. It's still home to major companies like Sunnen Products Company and has a busy Metrolink station. Like many other areas in and around St. Louis, Maplewood suffered a decline in the mid- to late-twentieth century as the population headed ever further

west. Happily, Maplewood has experienced a resurgence in recent years, especially along Manchester and Sutton roads, where the bulk of the city's restaurants, markets, and retailers are located.

While Brentwood only has a population of around 8,000, it has quite an economic base, with a variety of business calling the maze of offices and warehouses that comprise Hanley Industrial Court home. The city also boasts three popular shopping centers, Brentwood Promenade, Brentwood Square, and Dierbergs Brentwood Pointe.

Webster Groves, one of the oldest suburbs, was officially established in 1896 when the communities of Webster, Old Orchard, Webster Park, Tuxedo Park, and Selma combined. The city was promoted as a leafy green haven for those who wanted to escape the crowded urban environs of the city of St. Louis. One of the focal points of the community is Webster University, founded in 1915, which brings a diverse student population into the mix and contributes greatly to the economy. The Old Orchard District near the university and the downtown area a little further west along Big Bend Boulevard offer a wide variety of specialty shops and restaurants. Webster Groves also hosts a popular farmers market from May through October.

☐ BAUMANN'S FINE MEATS
baumannsfinemeats.com
8829 Manchester Rd.
Brentwood
314/968-3080
See entry on p. 125.

☐ MAPLEWOOD FARMERS MARKET
schlafly.com/bottleworks/farmers-market
Schlafly Bottleworks
7260 Southwest Ave.
Maplewood
Wednesdays, May–October, 4 p.m.–7 p.m.
See entry on p. 102.

☐ THE NATURAL WAY HEALTH FOOD
AND VITAMIN CENTERS
thenatway.com
8110 Big Bend Blvd.
Webster Groves
314/961-3541
See entry on p. 71.

☐ PENZEYS SPICES
penzeys.com
7338 Manchester Rd.
Maplewood
314/781-7177
See entry on p. 116.

☐ ROGER'S PRODUCE
625 E. Lockwood Ave.
Webster Groves
314/962-9157
See entry on p. 94.

☐ STRAUB'S
straubs.com
211 W. Lockwood Ave.
Webster Groves
314/962-0169
See entry on p. 58.

☐ VOM FASS
7314 Manchester Rd.
Maplewood
314/932-5262
See entry on p. 61.

☐ WEBSTER GROVES FARMERS
MARKET
webstergrovesfarmersmarket.com
Big Bend Blvd. and S. Old Orchard Ave.
Thursdays, May–October, 3 p.m.–6 p.m.
Webster Groves
See entry on p. 105.

**NOTES ON MAPLEWOOD, BRENTWOOD,
AND WEBSTER**

_____

_____

_____

_____

_____

_____

_____

_____

_____

_____

_____

KIRKWOOD, LADUE, AND FRONTENAC

The municipality of Kirkwood sprang up initially around the Pacific Railroad line and named after James Kirkwood, the railroad's chief engineer. In the mid-1800s, St. Louis was beset by trials and tribulations, from a cholera epidemic to a huge fire that destroyed a large portion of downtown. Folks were looking for a leafy green oasis to escape the travails of city life and with its railway station, Kirkwood seemed to fit the bill. In fact, it's considered to be the first planned suburb west of the Mississippi and became a proper city in 1865. Along with some of the county's finest examples of residential architecture, like the Mudd's Grove home, a three-story Greek Revival stunner at the corner of West Argonne Drive and North Harrison Avenue, Kirkwood is also home to one of the area's longest-running farmers markets, established in 1976.

Kirkwood's neighbors to the northwest, Ladue and Frontenac, also became refuges for those seeking solace from the urban grind. Wealthy St. Louisans migrated to these enclaves beginning in the early twentieth century and established some of the region's finest country clubs to keep themselves entertained, and a variety of private schools, like Chamonade Academy and St. Louis Country Day School, to educate their children. The rolling hills in these two towns are still home to plenty

of grand manses and gentile country estates, and it's easy to imagine red-jacketed riders on horseback hunting foxes over the hills and dales, as was the local custom in years past.

Both Ladue and Frontenac are rife with historical landmarks. One of the most notable in Ladue is the building at 9160 Clayton Road. Formerly the home of Busch's Grove restaurant, it first served as a stagecoach stop when it was built in the 1850s. Currently it's awaiting new occupants. For it's part, Frontenac boasts the Van Dyke home at 711 Oak Valley Drive built in 1854 and the Drum home on Spoede Road, built in 1860, among other sites. Frontenac sports the high-end shopping center Plaza Frontenac, anchored on either end by tony retailers Saks Fifth Avenue and Nieman-Marcus.

☐ **EXTRA VIRGIN: AN OLIVE OVATION**
extravirginoo.com
8829 Ladue Rd.
Ladue
314/727-6464
See entry on p. 54.

☐ **GLOBAL INTERNATIONAL**
globalfoodsmarket.com
421 N. Kirkwood Rd.
Kirkwood
314/835-1112
See entry on p. 220.

☐ KIRKWOOD FARMERS' MARKET

downtownkirkwood.com/farmers'-market.aspx
150 E. Argonne Dr.
Kirkwood
Mondays–Fridays, April–October, 9 a.m.–6 p.m.
Saturdays, April–October, 8 a.m. –5 p.m.
Limited hours for Thanksgiving/Christmas
holiday season
See entry on p. 101.

☐ LADUE MARKET

9155 Clayton Rd.
Ladue
314/993-0184
See entry on p. 81.

☐ RIVER CITY NUTRITION

833 S. Kirkwood Rd.
Kirkwood
314/822-1406
See entry on p. 72.

☐ SUR LA TABLE

surlatable.com
295 Plaza Frontenac
Frontenac
314/993-0566
See entry on p. 48.

☐ WILLIAMS-SONOMA

williams-sonoma.com
260 Plaza Frontenac
Frontenac
314/507-9211
See entry on p. 49.

NOTES ON KIRKWOOD, LADUE, AND FRONTENAC

_____
_____
_____
_____
_____
_____
_____
_____
_____
_____
_____
_____

UNIVERSITY CITY, OLIVETTE, AND OVERLAND

University City was founded in the early 1900s as the crown jewel in the personal empire of businessman—some would say ne'er-do-well—Edward Gerner Lewis. His plan was to headquarter his publishing empire there, develop private residential districts around his offices, create a town, and eventually install himself as its mayor. The city was incorporated in 1906 and Lewis named it University City because he intended it to be a center of culture and knowledge.

Lewis's dream did not last long—he left the area in 1912 with most of his empire in shambles and eventually made his way to California where he ended up in prison for fraud. But while he left his investors holding the bag, Lewis also left behind a legacy of eclectic and impressive architecture, like the octagonal building he used as his HQ at 6801 Delmar Boulevard (now the City Hall), and the pair of stone lions he commissioned to guard the entrance to his kingdom just a couple of blocks east from there on Delmar.

Today the area is best known for the Delmar Loop, a stretch of Delmar Boulevard that runs roughly from the aforementioned lions east to Skinker Boulevard, where it crosses the city limits. The Loop got its name because it was once the turnaround "loop" for the streetcar line, and today it's home to a plethora of restaurants, bars, shops, and entertainment venues. Most prominent of these is the Tivoli Theater, which is as ornate and splendid as it was when it opened in 1924. It still screens a variety of indie and mainstream films.

The population of U-City is fairly diverse, with an almost even split between black and white residents. Over the years its slightly offbeat vibe has been embraced by poets, musicians, punks, and other bohemian strains, though in recent times it has become much more gentrified and family-friendly, not nearly as seedy and scruffy as it once was. Of special note for visitors is the Walk of Fame. Much like that other celebrity-centric walkway in Hollywood, the U-City version, which runs up and down both sides of Delmar, features stars bearing the names and achievements of famous St. Louisans embedded in the concrete.

While the Loop gets most of the love when U-City is discussed, there is a lesser known but also interesting stretch just to the north on Olive Boulevard, brimming with Asian eateries and markets. This area segues into neighboring Olivette, which originally sprang up, along with adjacent Creve Coeur and Chesterfield, on what was known as The Road to Bon Homme Bottoms that ran between the Mississippi and Missouri rivers. What is now Olivette was the half-way point on this route, and the city still uses "in the center of it all" as its tagline on its official website. Olivette officially incorporated in 1930, the combination of four different communities, Central, Olive, Tower Hill, and Stratmann. It's wedged in between University City to the east and Creve Couer to the west and has a population just shy of 8,000. While it's small, Olivette does have plenty of amenities, starting with the five parks nestled within its borders.

Just a bit north lies Overland, another oft-overlooked muni, somewhat overwhelmed by the commercial crush of Page Avenue, which provides its southern border. Once you get off the commercial strip, though, Overland takes on the character of years past. Most of the streets feature rows of neat post-war bungalows, shotgun duplexes, and two-story brick homes reminiscent of many classic South City neighborhoods. The old downtown area on Woodson Road is lined with storefronts, evoking a time when the downtown area was a community's commercial center. For a fairly small city—population about 16,000 according to the last census—Overland has an abundance of green spaces, notably Wild Acres Park and Robert B. Brooks Park. It's also home to a thriving farmers market that operates on Saturdays from May to October.

☐ **AKBAR**
10606 Page Ave.
Olivette
314/428-1900
See entry on p. 197.

☐ **B & J PEERLESS RESTAURANT SUPPLY**
bjpeerless.com
1616 Dielman Rd.
Olivette
314/664-0400
See entry on p. 44.

☐ **BOB'S SEAFOOD**
bobsseafoodstl.com
8660 Olive Blvd.
Olivette
314/993-4844
See entry on p. 137.

☐ **CHINA TOWN MARKET**
8150 Olive Blvd.
Olivette
314/993-4303
See entry on p. 212.

☐ **EAST EAST ORIENTAL GROCERIES**
8619 Olive Blvd.
Olivette
314/432-5590
See entry on p. 213.

☐ **JALISCO MARKET**
Lotsie Depot Shopping Center
10086 Page Ave.
Overland
314/890-9898
See entry on p. 156.

☐ **KOHN'S KOSHER MARKET**
kohnskosher.com
10405 Old Olive Street Rd.
Olivette
314/569-0727
See entry on p. 55.

☐ **MALINTZI MEXICAN AND CENTRAL AMERICAN MARKET**
3831 Woodson Rd.
Overland
314/428-2075
See entry on p. 157.

☐ **MOUND CITY SHELLED NUT COMPANY**
moundcity.com
7831 Olive Blvd.
Olivette
314/725-9040
See entry on p. 56.

☐ **OLIVE FARMER'S MARKET (OLIVE SUPERMARKET)**
olivesupermarketstl.com/location.html
8041 Olive Blvd.
Olivette
314/997-5168
See entry on p. 215.

☐ **OVERLAND FARMERS MARKET**
overlandfarmersmarket.com
Overland Market Center
2500 block of Warson
Saturdays, May–October, 8 a.m.–12:30 p.m.
See entry on p. 102.

☐ SEAFOOD CITY GROCERY
7733 Olive Blvd.
Olivette
314/721-6688
See entry on p. 138.

☐ SEEMA ENTERPRISES & SEEMA
WORLD TRAVEL
10635 Page Ave.
Olivette
314/423-9990
See entry on p. 200.

☐ WINSLOW'S HOME AND FARM
winslowshome.com
7213 Delmar Blvd.
University City
314/725-7559
See entry on p. 84.

**NOTES ON UNIVERSITY CITY, OLIVETTE, AND
OVERLAND**

_____

_____

_____

_____

_____

_____

_____

_____

_____

_____

_____

_____

_____

CREVE COEUR

Creve Coeur was once considered to be "out in the country" by folks in the city proper. It began as a farming community some two hundred years ago. The first non-native settlers were French, followed by German immigrants, though archeological records indicate it was a thriving Native American enclave from about 9500 BC. Despite this long history, Creve Coeur didn't incorporate until 1949. Stories about the origin of the city's name—"broken heart" in French—vary. Some say it came from a Native American legend about a lovelorn princess, while other claim it's a reference to the early pioneers whose hearts broke because of the hardships they and their families suffered.

The area was sometimes known as Bon Homme, "good man" in French. After the city-county split in 1876, much of the area around Creve Coeur was referred to as Bon Homme Township. The city has come a long way from its humble beginnings—the current population is almost 18,000, and it's home to a range of commercial entities, including corporate giant Monsanto. While fully modern, Creve Couer still retains plenty of vestiges of its long and storied history. The Clester and Hackmann cabins, located in Conway Park, are both nearly two hundred years old and still standing for visitors to enjoy, as are the Lake School House, located in Lake School Park, and the Tappmayer farmhouse, which was moved to Millennium Park

in 2003, both of which date from the late 1800s.

Over the years, Creve Coeur has become an important place for the Jewish community in St. Louis. The city is home to the Jewish Community Center as well as the St. Louis Holocaust Museum and Learning Center (12 Millstone Campus Dr.).

☐ **ASIA MARKET**
Olive Blvd. and Fee Fee Rd.
Creve Coeur
See entry on p. 211.

☐ **THE NATURAL WAY HEALTH FOOD AND VITAMIN CENTERS**
thenatway.com
12345 Olive Blvd.
Creve Coeur
314/878-3001
See entry on p. 71.

☐ **THE WINE AND CHEESE PLACE**
wineandcheeseplace.com
457 N. New Ballas Rd.
Creve Coeur
314/989-0020
See entry on p. 146.

NOTES ON CREVE COEUR

_____

_____

_____

_____

_____

_____

MANCHESTER, BALLWIN, AND CHESTERFIELD

Sometimes it seems as though the municipalities of Manchester, Ballwin, and Chesterfield sprang up purely as a result of the flight to the suburbs that began in St. Louis in the mid-twentieth century. But these sections of west St. Louis County are as rich in history as any place within the city limits. The area that is now home to Manchester was reportedly first settled in the late 1700s by a French rifle maker named Migneron. Ballwin started out as a settlement around the home of farmer John Ball. Chesterfield supposedly derives its name from a visit to the area in the eighteenth century from a Lord Chesterfield of England, though it wasn't incorporated until 1988.

The rapid growth of these areas in recent years has produced a fair amount of strip malls, luxury car dealerships, and high-end residential developments with names that evoke the nature turned under and aside to create them. Chesterfield currently has a population of almost 48,000, making it the fourteenth largest city in the state. But while it might be easy to write off these areas as mere suburban sprawl, once you get off the major consumer trails like Manchester Road, it doesn't take long to get a sense of the beauty of the region and what makes it so attractive to those seeking a pastoral retreat from urban grit. Plenty of rolling tree-lined hills and shaded green spaces still flourish. Plus, historical sites exist and thrive amid the hustle and bustle of progress, such as the Barn at Lucerne in Ballwin (930 Kehrs Mill Rd.), currently an event space that was originally a pair of barns built with bricks left over from the 1904 World's Fair, and the Bacon Log Cabin (687 Henry Ave.), also in Ballwin, which has been restored and is open for tours courtesy of the Old Trails Historical Society. The restored Thornhill estate in Chesterfield's Faust Park (15185 Olive Blvd.) dates from around 1819 and includes the original home of Frederick Bates, the second governor of Missouri, and his family cemetery.

☐ MID-EAST MARKET
14345 Manchester Rd.
Ballwin
636/230-7018
See entry on p. 199.

☐ LA MORENA
14234 Manchester Rd.
Manchester Center
Ballwin
See entry on p. 158.

☐ SCHLAFLY BOTTLEWORKS
schlafly.com/bottleworks
7260 Southwest Ave.
Maplewood
314/241-BEER, x2
See entry on p. 145.

☐ SMOKEHOUSE MARKET
smokehousemarket.com
16806 Chesterfield Airport Rd.
Chesterfield
636/532-3314
See entry on p. 57.

☐ VIVIANO FESTA ITALIANO MARKET
vivianosmarket.com
150 Four Seasons Plz.
Chesterfield
314/878-1474
See entry on p. 187.

☐ WILLIAMS-SONOMA
williams-sonoma.com
277 Chesterfield Mall
Chesterfield
636/536-4370
See entry on p. 49.

☐ THE WINE AND CHEESE PLACE
wineandcheeseplace.com
14748 Clayton Rd.
Ballwin
636/227-49001
See entry on p. 146.

NOTES ON MANCHESTER, BALLWIN, AND CHESTERFIELD

_____

_____

_____

_____

_____

_____

_____

_____

_____

EQUIPMENT

There are many more one-use gadgets than functional tools out there—think avocado slicer, mushroom brush, grapefruit slicer—but once you have found a quality, helpful tool, it's a game changer. Trying to find the right tools can be a daunting task. How do you really know what's worth picking up? In an ideal world you could try out every tool on the shelves before buying it, but since that's not an option I've created a list of must-have tools for you—truly useful implements that can be purchased anywhere from our city's high-end cooking emporiums to its small Asian grocery stores. Consider restaurant supply stores, too. Most allow the public to come right in, wander around, and purchase the affordable industry-quality products they stock.

THE ONLY TEN PIECES OF EQUIPMENT YOU REALLY NEED

Any professional chef will tell you that the less *stuff* you have in the kitchen the better. More room to work and less clutter is more important than having a million different tools. Here are my recommendations for your kitchen and examples of their multiple uses.

☐ **CUTTING BOARD** – for cutting, resting, and displaying foods.

☐ **CHEF'S KNIFE** (I like an 8") – you can use one good-sized chef's knife for just about any job at all. I do have a paring knife in my kitchen, but mostly that's because it is easier to wash when I have little jobs.

☐ **MEDIUM CAST IRON SKILLET** – for sautéing, frying, baking, searing, roasting, and braising, a well-seasoned cast iron skillet is an extremely dynamic pan. And, it's the original non-stick skillet!

☐ **MEDIUM SAUCE POT WITH LID** – this size should suffice for all your cooking needs for up to six people. You may want to invest in a stock pot for large amounts of stock or soup, but go ahead and store it out of reach as you will most likely use it only rarely.

☐ **SMALL FOOD PROCESSOR** – don't spend hundreds of dollars and inches of counter space on a full size food processor. A mini processor stores easily, is a fraction of the cost, and the bowl's size (about three cups) is great for everyday processing (it fits about one can of beans, or just enough pesto for your pasta).

☐ **BLENDER** – there is only one way to really make food really smooth— blenders are necessary for velvety soups, smooth pasta sauces, and making nut milks or smoothies.

☐ **TONGS** – all you need to move, flip, toss, and handle any food.

☐ **WOODEN SPOON** – the simple utensil that's both functional and beautiful. Use wooden spoons for stirring, serving, and sautéing. They're better for your pans, your health, and your soul than plastic or metal counterparts.

☐ **MESH STRAINER** – there's no real substitute for this specific tool. It makes so many jobs painless and easy.

☐ **GRATER** – finally, no style of chopping will ever achieve what a grater can do. Apply today to cheese, onions, potatoes, chocolate…

What other delights for enhancing your kitchen and its activities are you likely to find at the stores in this chapter?

CARING FOR YOUR CAST IRON

Folklore dictates that every bride should receive a cast iron skillet and a rolling pin to guarantee a successful marriage. Feed your family *and* keep them in line.

In my house, the cast iron skillets and Dutch oven are the most frequently used cookware. They are heavy-duty, they heat evenly and hold the heat, they are oven safe, and they are a cinch to clean when seasoned properly.

Proper seasoning of cast iron seems to boggle the modern mind, which is why can you find so many rusted cast iron skillets at thrift stores. Seasoning of cast iron may be lost art, but it's an easy one to learn.

First, whether a pan is dusty, sticky, or rusty, all it needs is a thorough scrubbing with a metal scrub pad. (I use the stainless steel scrubbers that you can find at restaurant supply stores, but any coarse metal scrub pads *without* the built-in soap will do). Using a lot of elbow grease—and a *tiny* touch of soap only if needed—scrub the pan inside and out until the rust and grease are gone.

Once your pan is scoured, dry it by placing it on a lit burner. After the pan cools down, rub the outside and the inside generously with cooking oil (corn or vegetable), then pour enough oil in the pan to cover the bottom. Place pan in the oven at 500° for fifteen minutes, then reduce heat to 200° for three more hours. Leave the pan in the oven with the heat off until it cools (or overnight), then remove it and pour off excess oil.

Voilà—a well-seasoned cast iron skillet!

Now comes the tricky part: keeping it well-seasoned. Cast irons are generally easier to clean once they've cooled, so they're usually the last dish I tend to. Using the same type of steel scrubber used to season the pan, scrub it with hot water and nothing else. If your pan is well-seasoned, everything will slip right off. *Do not use soap!* Soap will undo the seasoning and make everything stick to it again. *Do not leave your pan soaking!* Soaking your cast iron also will undo the seasoning and will even rust it.

A cast iron skillet is like every other tool in your house. Take care of it properly and it will take care of you. Happy cooking.

SMALL EQUIPMENT

- [ ] **CAST IRON COOKWARE** – perhaps the most reliable and versatile of cookware options, it's necessary to have at least one piece in your collection.
- [ ] **CAMBROS** – plastic containers of just about every size with tight-fitting lids, perfect for storing and transporting anything.
- [ ] **CHINOIS** –fine mesh conical strainers, good for straining stock and sauces.
- [ ] **CHEF'S KNIVES** – I generally prefer the German (Wusthof or Henckels) or Japanese (Global or Shun) varieties, but you can find sturdy, inexpensive knives at any restaurant supply store.

☐ **CITRUS JUICERS** – the best thing to come out of Mexico since salsa, these hinged juicers deliver all the juice and none of the seeds.

☐ **CUTTING BOARDS** – in all sizes and materials, though bamboo or wood are best. And never cut on the glass ones.

☐ **HALF, FOURTH, THIRD, SIXTH, AND NINTH HOTEL PANS** – smaller versions of the hotel pans (see below), wonderful go-to pans for cooking or storing food, available in metal or plastic, and in varying depths.

☐ **HOTEL PANS** – also called "full pans," these metal wonders can be essential for cooking large items in the oven. Inexpensive and durable, they're definitely worth the money. You can also find them in plastic—great for toting things to that large family gathering.

☐ **IMMERSION BLENDERS** – handy tools well-suited for puréeing hot things—a lot cleaner and faster than using standup blenders.

☐ **MANDOLINES** – hand-held slicers ideal for slicing vegetables exquisitely thin, I prefer the Asian ones to the European ones. The Asian versions are made of plastic, but are usually sharper and easier to use. Plus, their blades are removable for sharpening.

☐ **MICROPLANES** – these fine graters are what you want for zesting citrus or grating chocolate and hard cheeses.

☐ **PARCHMENT PAPER** – much better than wax paper, it keeps your cookie sheets clean as a whistle.

☐ **PASTRY BAGS** – convenient for icing cakes and other fun decorating projects.

☐ **PASTRY BRUSHES** – make for easy brushing of butter and sauces.

☐ **PROFESSIONAL APPLIANCES** – pro appliances simply work better and longer than retail brands, though they may not always look as sleek.

  • **blenders** – nothing beats a nice blender, for making everything from smoothies to creamy soups.

  • **food processors** – a good quality food processor can last a lifetime. Look for a heavy-duty motor and well-made attachments.

  • **rice cookers** –I love these—not only do they cook rice to perfection every time, but they keep it warm for hours to boot. Who doesn't need to take the guess work and tough cleanup out of cooking rice?

☐ **SHEET TRAYS** – thicker and sturdier than conventional cookie sheets, and a must-have (let's make them #11 on my list). Available in ½ and ¼ sizes too.

☐ **SPATULAS (HEAT PROOF)** – the perfect tools for stirring anything in a hot pot, much sturdier than consumer-grade ones.

☐ **SPEED POURS** – small plastic or metals gadgets that fit on the top of liquor (or other) bottles for cleaner, better pouring. Get some for your olive oils and vinegars.

☐ **STAINLESS STEEL BOWLS** – attractive, durable, and sold in umpteen sizes.

☐ **TONGS** – best tool for picking things up, hands down.

☐ **WOODEN SPOONS** – they come in all shapes and sizes, are kinder to your cookware, and won't react with food like metal implements. I personally own fifteen different shaped wooden spoons in my kitchen—my newest find, the flat-edged spoon.

SMALL EQUIPMENT SHOPPING LIST/NOTES

_____

_____

_____

_____

_____

_____

_____

_____

_____

_____

LARGE EQUIPMENT

☐ **BARSTOOLS** – a great addition to any kitchen, definitive counter seating for the kids or your friends to park themselves while you cook.

☐ **BUTCHER BLOCK TABLES** – a super choice if you have the space, these make for a robust and attractive work station and they double as a cutting board.

☐ **STAINLESS STEEL PREP TABLES** – nothing like having a big work space!

☐ **STAINLESS STEEL SINKS** – easy to clean and hard-wearing.

LARGE EQUIPMENT SHOPPING LIST/NOTES

_____

_____

_____

_____

_____

_____

_____

_____

_____

_____

"A SHARP KNIFE IS A SAFE KNIFE."

Plenty of culinary wisdom has been passed on through the generations, but this is one of the most important. A knife is usually your first and most essential tool. Taking proper care of it makes cooking much easier. Struggling with a dull knife can not only be frustrating, but also downright dangerous.

A dull knife is more prone to slipping and sliding on the food or the board. When you chop with a sharp blade, it goes straight through the food and hits the board, keeping your fingers safe. That also means extra control, and extra control means greater confidence. Your skills are sure to improve with a sharp knife.

If worse comes to worse, and you do cut yourself, a cut from a sharp blade is much cleaner and heals much faster than one from a dull knife.

The two places I know of in the metro area that sharpen knives besides Schuncks are The Kitchen Conservatory (see p. 47) and Bertarelli (see p. 45). Keeping your knives sharp is cheaper than your think, three knives should be under $15.

STORES

B & J PEERLESS RESTAURANT SUPPLY
bjpeerless.com
1616 Dielman Rd.
Olivette
314/664-0400

The name tells the truth: There is nowhere else in St. Louis like Peerless Restaurant Supply for the public to get their hands on restaurant equipment. It truly is without equal. No overpriced store with a crappy selection—it is the real deal.

For almost twenty years it was located on Grand Boulevard, serving restaurants and the public alike. About eight years ago they moved right off of Page on Dielman Road in Olivette to take over a huge warehouse space. This move took Peerless from being a big, fun place to shop to a gigantic, fun place to shop. The building is filled to the rafters with every piece of equipment you need or want and don't yet know you need or want. Have a remotely culinary whim, dream, or project—to deck out your home bar or start a curbside cotton candy business? Yep, this joint's for you.

Peerless carries all the restaurant industry essentials: those metal bowls you drool over on every cooking show, and plastic containers that kick Tupperware out the door. Here you can find hotel pans (in all the sizes, both plastic and metal), mid-grade knives, cutting boards, thermometers, speed pours, bar mats, skillets, tongs, just about anything in small or large equipment category (refrigerators, stoves, and freezers too). Relive your glory days as a college server, or bring the essence of the Food Network into your kitchen. Whatever your vision or motivation, they can set you up.

Wait, there's more. There's a huge selection of china, glassware, and flatware. Remember those thick mugs from breakfast at the Parkmore (an old drive-in demolished about ten years back)? You can find ones just like them here. They sell adjustable metal shelving (called metro shelves) perfect for your garage and basement storage, or even your kitchen. Score incredible finds in their bargain section.

Everything in the store is of restaurant quality, which works if you need to feed a crowd or simply want practical kitchen supplies that will endure years of wear and tear. The staff can be counted on to be helpful and patient with you lay folks, so feel free to stop in and look around. Even if you're not in the market for anything (really?), make a point to come sometime for the browsing adventure.

BERTARELLI CUTLERY
bertarellicutlery.com
1927 Marconi Ave.
The Hill
314/664-4005

John Bertarelli knows all the secrets of the restaurants in this town, as he finds himself in dozens of kitchens a week for about ten minutes at a time. John and his family keep the knives of St. Louis restaurant kitchens hair-splittingly sharp. Their drop-off service is an integral part of keeping the wheels turning at big and small establishments alike. The boys of the Bertarelli family have been sharpening knives for restaurants since 1967, so we can be sure of two things: the Bertarellis know a heck of a lot about knives and they are privy to lots of good food industry gossip.

The Bertarelli brick-and-mortar store on The Hill is the foremost place to have your personal knives sharpened. These gentlemen offer "while you wait" sharpening service (if they aren't too busy), so you can browse the store while you wait. Or just drop them off for next-day pickup.

Family-owned and immensely enjoyable, Bertarelli is *the place* to talk knives. I need that outlet, don't you? The front half of the store is stocked with a vast array of nicely affordable kitchen equipment (some refurbished), most restaurant quality, as well was small equipment like spatulas, pepper grinders, baking equipment, and, obviously, knives. They sell full lines of Wusthof, Global, Shun, Forschner, and Dexter Russell knives, as well as the locally-produced, handcrafted NHB Knife Works.

The back half of this store is the open-air sharpening studio. It is super interesting to see the tools of the trade all laid out and watch the guys at work. All in all, it is a sheer joy to shop and do business here, and, if you listen closely, you just might get some dirt on your favorite restaurant.

DIGREGORIO'S ITALIAN FOODS
5200 Daggett Ave.
The Hill
314/776-1062
See entry on p. 184.

FORD HOTEL AND RESTAURANT SUPPLY
fordstl.com
2204 N. Broadway
North Downtown
314/231-8400 or 800/472-3673

Located on the mostly industrial part of Broadway, Ford is open to the public and a fantastic place for restaurant supply store beginners. Walk up a huge flight of stairs and the site opens to two showrooms. The showroom on the right is filled with ovens, ranges, aluminum pots, anti-fatigue mats (for periods of extended standing), thermometers, spatulas, and all manner of small equipment. The showroom on the left houses rows and rows of plates, bowls, flatware, and glassware, all of it restaurant quality. Browse the shelves of square bowls, triangular plates, and candy-colored bowls. Swoon over simple and classy embossed dishware. Grab yourself unbreakable wine glasses and kid-proof tumblers.

The complete array of glassware is almost beyond description, but I am sure 1) that they have what you are looking for, and 2) the selection will tickle drink-ware needs and wants you haven't yet discovered. Go green with sturdy clear plastic diner cups for backyard parties, serve your next dessert in classic bulb snifters, entertain the girls with over-the-top martini glasses, impress with simple heavy bottomed rocks glasses...I could digress like this for hours.

The expert staff can help you select tiny ceramic dishes for a tableful of condiments: dainty ovals, little frying pans, and fluted ramekins, oh my. After you have chosen your interestingly patterned or unusually shaped plates, move on to determining just which lovely oven-proof dish will debut at your next dinner, filled with cassoulet or a personal pot pie.

KITCHEN CONSERVATORY

kitchenconservatory.com
8021 Clayton Rd.
Clayton
314/862-2665 or 886/862-2433

This place is a home cook's paradise, full of gadgets, books, all the necessary tools, and interesting equipment galore. You have questions, these ladies have answers! They are just about the most knowledgeable and accommodating staff in the city, not only about what they sell but anything and everything food related.

Above all, Kitchen Conservatory is especially well-stocked when it comes to baking equipment—resplendent with cookie cutters, rolling pins, pans in various shapes and sizes, layers of cookie sheets, pastry bags, decorating tools, and Magic Line pans. It is a baker's wonderland complete with the most adorable cupcake cups and stands to boot.

Notably, Kitchen Conservatory is the only store in town to carry a full line of Magic Line pans. These are professional quality pans, but certainly used by the serious home baker. They are made of heavy gauge aluminum, which will never warp or stain and heats evenly. The sides of these pans are at a ninety-degree angle to the bottom, which makes it easier to loosen the product inside. For even greater ease, all the pans have versions with removable bottoms.

Along with the baking equipment you can find a divine assortment of cutting boards, gorgeous utensils, gourmet ingredients and specialty food items, a full line of Republic of Tea teas, fancy condiments, three lines of Wusthof knives, just about every small appliance that Cuisinart makes, and stunning Le Crueset Cookware. Sigh. They carry frozen parbaked Companion loaves that are ready for the oven, along with delicious Plugrá Butter (a gourmet European brand). Suffice it to say, you won't look at bread and butter at home the same again.

Two open kitchen classrooms reside in the back half of the store. One classroom is intimate, seating about twenty people around a counter facing a well-stocked kitchen. The other has a huge marble island for hands-on cooking classes, where students get their hands messy cooking and learning.

Kitchen Conservatory hosts classes daily—about 800(!) a year and fairly affordable too—taught by professional chefs/restaurateurs as well as in-house culinary educators. These classes range from basic knife skills and holiday baking to Italian classics and vegan cooking. I have been both a teacher and a guest in many classes, and, let me tell you, there is no better way to spend an evening, a ladies lunch, or a Saturday morning than cooking and eating with like-minded folks. These offerings combine restaurant quality food with an unforgettable learning experience. Search the class list on their website by subject, day, or even your favorite St. Louis chef.

Kitchen Conservatory also offers next-day knife sharpening services every day they're open but one—the Wednesday before Thanksgiving. That's the day you can have your knife sharpened while you wait! Whew.

There are a few items available at only this store: a gnocchi board crafted by a local woodworker with local wood, a wooden-handled turkey lifter (ask about it), and gingerbread house cookie cutters, custom-made especially for this store. My favorite part of Kitchen Conservatory is the wall of Mason jars in all sizes and shapes, just beckoning for a canning project. So skip asking Google and run into Kitchen Conservatory for a real culinary education.

OLIVE FARMERS MARKET
8041 Olive Blvd.
See entry on p. 215.

SUR LA TABLE
surlatable.com
295 Plaza Frontenac
Frontenac
314/993-0566

My pet interpretation of Sur La Table is "the average person's Williams-Sonoma"—it has a lot more gadgets and is a little less expensive. That, to me, makes it much more fun to shop here. This is the place for those one-use tools we don't need but we tend to like: avocado knives, mango cutters, cherry pitters. When you get over using them, they can spend the rest their lives delightfully clanging around in your kitchen drawer.

Sur La Table is a full-service kitchen equipment store, complete with cookie cutters and whisks and cutting boards. First created in Seattle in 1972 in Pike Place Market, it's now a national chain with over one hundred locations. It does have that chain vibe and it is located in a mall, but that doesn't detract from a remarkable selection.

They have a beautiful line of cast iron cookware, and full lines of chef's knives (Wusthof, Henkels, Shun, and Global), along with tea kettles and espresso makers, a large amount of pastry and baking equipment, tools, spices, sauces in jars, teas, and soap. It's hard to miss Sur La Table's five different Le Crueset color lines, all of which would add a dazzling pop of color to your kitchen.

To review: There's a wealth of small treasures here, and that makes it a dependable place to pick up little holiday or birthday presents.

EL TORITO
2753 Cherokee St.
South St. Louis
314/771-8648
See entry on p. 159.

WILLIAMS-SONOMA
williams-sonoma.com
260 Plaza Frontenac
Frontenac
314/507-9211

277 Chesterfield Mall
Chesterfield
636/536-4370

I'm sure you have seen the glossy pages of a Williams-Sonoma catalog. Going into the store is just like stepping into those pages. Every shiny gadget, sturdy appliance, herb-scented soap, and soft linen napkin summoning you from the catalog is here in all three magnificent dimensions.

W-S is very cookware heavy. They carry a full line of brightly colored Le Crueset Dutch ovens and jewel-toned Emilie Henry pie pans and casserole dishes, whose beauty is surpassed only by their strength and functionality. Start or complete your set of polished Calphalon or All-Clad pots and pans here. You can even pick up a pot rack to display a gorgeous set of Mauviel Copper, the French cookware known for its lustrous glow and efficient temperature control. If you can't afford it, don't forget…Williams-Sonoma has a bridal registry!

Of course, no kitchen (or kitchen store) is complete without chef's knives, and they do have every sort of blade Wusthof, Henkels, Shun, and Global make.

The consummate staff can point you in the direction of elegant cookbooks, inspired table linens, and rarefied condiments, or walk you through the minutia of the ten types of espresso makers they stock. Williams-Sonoma is one of the oldest names in kitchenware and is still in the running as one of the best.

STORES NOTES

_____

_____

_____

_____

_____

_____

_____

_____

_____

_____

GOURMET AND SPECIALTY FOODS

Gourmet stores are cosmopolitan havens for hard-to-find, high-quality, imported and domestic goods. As our populace (locally and nationally) gets more sophisticated, we see more of these items in the mega groceries, but that hardly makes these food boutiques obsolete. These stores are typically small with enlightened staff and customer service. This affords you the luxuries of having your questions answered in nitty-gritty depth as well as amenities like special ordering items you can't find elsewhere.

Specialty stores fall under the gourmet category, but generally specialize in a narrow range of foodstuffs. Run by someone with a clear passion for food and cooking, these stores and their proprietors inspire me and can be even more exciting to visit.

INGREDIENTS AND PRODUCTS

This list of ingredients you'll find at such shops is by no means complete, but I've highlighted my favorites and what I know to be appealing and useful to others.

ALMOND FLOUR – a tasty addition to baked items and a charming breading for fish.

ARBORIO RICE – a short grain, glutinous rice used for making risotto, and great for rice puddings as well.

CHEESES – imported and domestic, innumerable varieties and variations.

CHOCOLATE – high quality and high-percentage dark.

CRÈME FRAÎCHE – a less sour version of sour cream, delightful for desserts or soups.

DRY PORCINIS, PORCINI POWDER – fresh porcinis are prohibitively expensive, but dried whole or powdered is a sufficient substitute and retain much of their flavor.

DUCK FAT – a delicious addition to any dish that requires fat (imagine a roux with duck fat) or for making your own confit.

FARRO – a hearty Mediterranean grain, with a chewy texture and packed with vitamins.

FLEUR DE SEL – extra fancy sea salt not used for cooking but for finishing a dish. Sprinkle a very small amount on freshly baked cookies for amazing flavor.

MUSTARDS – the types are seemingly limitless.

NUTS (WALNUTS, PINE NUTS, ALMONDS, AND PECANS, FOR STARTERS) – sold in bulk or prepackaged; roasted, raw, salted, or smoked; whole, chopped, or otherwise sliced and diced.

OILS (WALNUT, TRUFFLE, AVOCADO, ALMOND, PINE NUT, PISTACHIO, GRAPE SEED, MUSTARD OIL, RICE BRAN OIL) – so many to choose from, some for cooking and some for salads.

PASTA – Can I say oodles of noodles? Fresh and dry, in all shapes and flavors. Look for the locally-made pastas, too.

PURE MAPLE SYRUP – expensive, sure, but the flavor is worth the investment.

SALAMI AND OTHER PRESERVED MEAT – the Italian influence on this town has made these products widely available.

STOCKS AND BASES – there are only a few very high quality stocks and bases out there. Try to avoid the ones with ingredients you can't pronounce.

VANILLA POWDER – the entire bean, dried and ground, leaving flavor intact when heated (unlike vanilla extract) and a supreme choice for baking.

VINEGARS (FLAVORED AND INFUSED) – as there are many, many types, it's always a good time to try one you've never had.

INGREDIENTS AND PRODUCTS NOTES

_____

_____

_____

_____

_____

_____

_____

_____

STORES

EXTRA VIRGIN, AN OLIVE OVATION
extravirginoo.com
8829 Ladue Rd.
Ladue
314/727-6464

Stepping into Extra Virgin, I expected to find shelf after shelf of olive oil and maybe some olives and sun-dried tomatoes. I couldn't have been more wrong. Olive oil actually comprises only a small percentage of their inventory, all of which is hand-picked by owner Marianne Prey, M.D. These jewels of the packaged food world—honeys, vinegars, crackers, truffles, salts, mustards, dry pasta, and the like—are chosen for the quality of their ingredients as well as their ability to complement the oils in stock.

Much like wine, olive oil and vinegar production are affected by a growing season, *terroir* (the soil and geographical conditions under which things are grown), aging methods, and attention to detail. Phrases like "fruitiness and floral notes," "500-year-old Orleans method," and "aged in oak barrels" came up when Cameron, a store employee, handed me samples of vinegar. I got seriously schooled that day. Marianne opened Extra Virgin after years of medical practice and studying the benefits of olive oil. With obvious passion in her voice, she described to me the methods of the Katz Vineyard, a family-owned olive oil and vinegar producer from California: "unlike most vinegar producers, Katz actually grows their own grapes, makes their own wine, and then ferments their vinegars." Now that's love.

EVOO not only has a beautiful selection of refined products for your tastebuds, but beautiful things to look at too—gorgeous olive wood utensils, brightly patterned ceramic platters, colorful linens, and carefully vetted cookbooks. This store started in a small storefront in Clayton not too long ago. The new, bigger store in Ladue bumped their space up to 400 square feet with some of that dedicated to classes and sit down events. Marianne proudly informed me that they were able to greatly increase all their wonderful inventory, including oils that are not from olives. So go in and get educated in olive pressing and grape fermentation. Or, sit back and have it delivered in the form of a seasonally themed baskets from their Olive Ovations Club, complete with a range of products, a history and description of each, and useful recipes. Doctor's orders.

KOHN'S KOSHER MARKET
kohnskosher.com
10405 Old Olive Street Rd.
Olivette
314/569-0727

Kosher food is raised, processed, and prepared according to Jewish dietary laws. Simply put, these laws are: no mixing of dairy with meat, only eating meat from herbivorous birds or from animals with cloven hooves, only eating meat slaughtered and prepared with the utmost care and sanitation, and only eating seafood if it is has both fins and scales (i.e., basically fish).

Many non-Jews enjoy kosher foods for ethical and health reasons. They find kosher slaughtering methods more humane, kosher ingredients more natural, and kosher sanitation regulations surpassing all others. Kosher meat can't even be frozen, so it is generally extremely fresh.

Kohn's is the premier, and now only, kosher grocery in St. Louis. Its butcher offers a full selection of beef and chicken cuts, freshly butchered. There's also an impressive selection of frozen appetizers, spinach pies, tabouleh, couscous, soups, sauces, olive oil, cheese, and pickles; an active deli counter; and an ample prepared foods section. Prepared foods include things like orzo salad, caponata, broiled fish, potato salad, and baked chicken, and a number of things prepared for you to take home and cook there—lasagna, macaroni and cheese, and eggplant parmesan, to name a few.

Do remember when going here that they are closed on Saturday for Sabbath.

LADUE MARKET
9155 Clayton Rd.
Ladue
314/993-0184
See entry on p. 81.

LOCAL HARVEST GROCERY
localharvestgrocery.com
3148 Morganford Rd.
Tower Grove South
314/865-5260
See entry on p. 82.

MOUND CITY SHELLED NUT COMPANY
7831 Olive Blvd.
Olivette
314/725-9040

This little store is packed full of nuts! Mound City has been roasting nuts since 1917, and selling out of their Olive Boulevard location for thirty-eight years. The husband and wife team that own Mound City have many years of family history tied into these nuts, and more specifically, their chocolate confections. When the Kessells first bought the company in 1973 they got help from a grandfather who hand-dipped chocolates, and they have continued the tradition ever since.

No surprise, you can find all types of nuts (almonds, cashews, peanuts, macadamias, walnuts) here in all sorts of conditions (raw, salted, roasted, roasted and salted, sweetened, chocolate covered). You can purchase nuts individually by the pound or choose from a vast array of gift boxes and party trays. Other than nuts, Mound City sells candy, popcorn, dried fruit, and even chocolate covered strawberries. All their nuts are kosher, as are almost ninety percent of their other products. Note to self and to you: holiday gifts and party favors!

Two personal recommendations: Try their delicious chocolate peanut butter, made fresh with 100% peanuts and dark chocolate. Ask about the Microwave Peanuts; you will not be disappointed.

PARKER'S TABLE
parkerstable.com
7118 Oakland Ave
Clayton
314/645-2050

The brightly lit and warmly painted Parker's Table is a great new, yet old, addition to the St. Louis food and beverage landscape, happily situated right at the culmination of the city line, Clayton, and Richmond Heights. Owner, Jonathan Parker is excited to have the new space with tons of… well…space. Opened almost two decades ago, Parker's Table recently took a three-year hiatus that ended last year with the opening of the new store.

The commitment to wine here is obvious from the racks and racks and shelves and even temperature-controlled rooms of carefully selected vintages. But what might be less obvious is that it is a wine store with a foodie attitude. Housed under the gorgeous tin ceiling and behind the huge plate glass windows is a diverse cross section of specialty and local food products like chocolate, coffee, tea, cheese, oils, and vinegars. The source of most pride (besides the wine) seems to be the pasta selection, various shapes and sizes are out in bins, ready to be weighed out, taken home, and turned into a delicious pairing for your new bottle of wine.

But Parker's Table doesn't just stop at wine, they have a beer and liquor selection to swoon over. They host regular tasting in their generous tasting space along with fun other community events, like knitting classes, wine themed craft workshops, and home brewer competitions. Come to Parker's Table for gifts (for yourself or others), to support local businesses, and—most importantly—to find the most congenial wine shopping in the city. The staff strive to make your wine buying experience easy, transparent, and even fun! When asked what he wishes people knew about wine by *Feast Magazine*, the owner responded, "How easy it is!" Go see how easy it is.

PENZEYS SPICES
penzeys.com
7338 Manchester Rd.
Maplewood
314/781-7177
See entry on p. 116.

SMOKEHOUSE MARKET
smokehousemarket.com
16806 Chesterfield Airport Rd.
Chesterfield
636/532-3314

This is one of my favorite finds researching for this book. I walked in and first thing I said to myself was, "How have you lived without this place before?" The Smokehouse Market is a small room packed full of wonderful things to eat and cook.

Their specialty, as the name indicates, is smoked and/or preserved meat. Let's itemize some of just their house-made delicacies: raw sausages (bratwurst, Hungarian chorizo, knackwurst, Italian, breakfast links), bacon, summer sausage, veal sausage, braunschweiger, salami, pastrami, corned beef, and smoked tongue. It doesn't end there—you can find a plethora of ready-to-cook beef, pork, and chicken in about every cut imaginable, as well as fully cooked barbeque (pulled pork, pulled brisket, pork steaks, and ribs).

The deli coolers are full of good-looking preparations, such as potato salad, tuna salad, chicken salad, broccoli salad, green bean salad, coleslaw, tomato salad, and pasta salad. The produce is minimal (basics mostly—potatoes, lettuce, carrots, etc.), but what they do have is terrific (they had striking heirloom tomatoes when I was last there). Their cheese selection? Fabulous.

Smokehouse Market also stocks a decent array of frozen seafood, including tilapia, tuna, salmon, shrimp, crab cakes, and anchovies. The rest of the store doesn't disappoint with its stock of gourmet and hard-to-find groceries. Expect high-quality chocolate, ice cream, olive oils, crackers, chips, and many types of butter, candies, and dry pasta, and an enormous selection of house-made goodies like dips, sauces, salsas, quick breads, pies, and cookies. Give the gift of Smokehouse with a nice gift basket.

This wonderful little catch is located next to Annie Gunn's restaurant, and also sells the restaurant's retail sauces and other specialties.

STRAUB'S
straubs.com
302 N. Kingshighway Blvd.
Central West End
314/361-6646

8282 Forsyth Blvd.
Clayton
314/725 2121

211 W. Lockwood Ave.
Webster Groves
314/962-0169

13414 Clayton Rd.
Town and Country
314/434-4707

The first Straub's opened in Webster Groves in 1901. Later, they added locations in Clayton in 1933, Central West End in 1948, Town and Country in 1966, and most recently an online store.

Straub's: a gourmet food shopper's heaven. Each store differs slightly, but each offers a full line of groceries, including kosher, vegan, organic, and gluten-free products. Each store has a bakery, a butcher (full line of beef, chicken, and pork—some of it already marinated for you), a seafood counter (a huge selection of fresh fish, complete with live lobsters), a deli counter with prepared foods (great for picking something up on the way home from work), a florist, a great selection of produce, and even some small kitchen equipment. They also sell wine, beer, greeting cards, and pet food.

Straub's beautifully smokes meat for holidays and every day. Each store carries over one hundred specialty sodas, root beers, and sparkling waters. They're known for their chicken salad and offer, what they call "casual catering," at all stores. This includes box lunches, deli trays, appetizers, and entrées. And, with off-the-shelf sampling, these stores are truly full service.

SUGAREE BAKING
1242 Tamm Ave.
Dogtown
314/645-5496

Named after a Grateful Dead song, this adorable storefront bakery owned by a few hippies-turned-legit has graced Tamm Avenue in Dogtown for almost twenty years. The building was built over a hundred years ago for a bakery run by the Keis Family and has remained a bakery ever since.

Sugaree is decked out with marble counters, pies resting on classic glass stands, and a playful tile mosaic out front. While you certainly can and should buy pies, cookies, and cakes there, the store also serves as a wedding cake show room.

Best known for their wedding cakes and pies, Pat and Jim, the charming wife-husband duo that own and run the joint, use their art backgrounds and love of food to make their sugary desserts delicious and beautiful. (Let me emphasize: their cakes aren't just for weddings. Let Pat design a unique creation for whatever event you might be planning.) The cakes, mousses, buttercreams, and ganaches are all made in house with real butter and whole, fresh eggs— nothing fake in this holy house of sweet things.

Owner Jimmy has re-awakened his chef skills of late to create well-crafted pot pies that are gaining in popularity. The full-of-home-cooked-goodness beef and chicken pies are made from scratch (like, Jimmy even makes homemade stock first) and sold frozen out of the storefront.

The sweet pie fillings change weekly. Reawaken childhood whimsy with their fluffy Chocolate Cream Pie, make-your-grandma-smile Apple Caramel Crumb, or you-can-tell-yourself-it's-good-for-you Berries of the Forest. And you can always supplement a pie purchase with cookies! Shortbread, teacake, sugar, biscotti...

VOLPI ITALIAN SALAMI & MEAT COMPANY
volpifoods.com
5263 Northrup
The Hill
314/772-8550

One step into the small Volpi storefront, one whiff, and you realize that after a hundred years of making salami on The Hill, they've still got it. The intermingling smells of cured meats and pungent cheeses envelop you. Volpi's success strategy seems twofold—hold onto the original recipes *and* revitalize the old ways. Perfect example: Their newest line of all natural salamis is made from Missouri Beef, without chemical preservatives, and infused with wine.

Volpi's cramped quarters presents a feast of salamis and other cured meats, including sopressata, filzette, coppa, bresaola, capicola, hot sopressa, romano salame, proscuitto, Genova salame, and pancetta. *All of which you can taste before buying.* You will find yourself searching for recipes and excuses to use these cured meats—and eating a lot more sandwiches. For the thrifty shopper, they offer ends and extras for cheap.

Beyond meats, they have plenty of domestic and imported cheeses, mostly Italian: asiago for your cheese bread, parmesan for your pasta, and mozzarella for your eggplant. The nice folks working the store will slice both the meat and cheese to order, then wrap it in old-school butcher paper. And I swear, there is something about their cheese...phenomenal.

Store shelves round out the Italian offerings—briny olives, pine nuts, crisp biscotti, extra virgin and pomace olive oil, vinegars, dried porcinis, dry pasta, frozen tortellini and ravioli.

This is definitely the place to go to create an antipasto platter to wow your Italian in-laws.

VOM FASS
7314 Manchester Rd.
Maplewood
314/932-5262

A number of years ago, this European company opened its first U.S. store in St. Louis, right in the heart of Maplewood. Part of the recent Maplewood rejuvenation, Vom Fass adds some culinary cred to the now hopping Manchester strip by offering anything that comes "from the cask," which is the literal translation of their name.

Oil and vinegar, check. But let's jump for a minute to the scotch, Irish whisky, wine, and a number of liquors all kept in beautiful wood casks that line the walls of the store. From the casks you can sample each offering (note: you can serve yourself, but an employee won't leave your side while you're there) or simply fill one of the *forty* varieties of glass bottles they have for sale. There's a small half-pint bottle perfect for host/hostess gifts and tall, thin corked bottles attractive for displaying. They even have torso-shaped bottles. More brandy, grappa, rum, absinthe, and fruit and nut flavored liqueurs round out the liquor selection. These come in a range of sizes, many in decorative bottles, and make choice presents.

Back to an oil selection that basically puts every other store to shame—they not only have fine extra virgin olive oils but a multitude of nut, seed, infused, and what they call "wellness" oils. The extremely friendly and informed staff supplies opulent descriptions of the flavors, textures, and "terroir" of each extra virgin olive oil when providing a small sample. The subtly flavored seed oils include sesame, grape seed, and rapeseed—all nice for cooking—as well as argan and pumpkin seed, which work well as finishing oils. The nut oils include almond, pistachio, hazelnut, and walnut—all delicate and best used for salad dressings or as finishing oils (even on desserts). "Wellness" oils are comprised of cumin, primrose, flax, and wheat germ—some good for cooking, some for your skin, and some as nutritional supplements.

The vinegar barrels here are filled with balsamics and vinegars made with fruit, wine, champagne, herbs, honey, and ginger. You will be astounded when you begin to grasp the complexity of an aged balsamic, or try fruit vinegar on your ice cream as the staff advocates.

The smells, tastes, descriptions, sensory input that is Vom Fass are downright tantalizing, making it almost impossible to ever go back to flat olive oil and boring vinegar. Your salad dressing will thank you.

WINSLOW'S HOME AND FARM
7213 Delmar Blvd.
University City
314/725-7559
See entry on p. 84.

GOURMET AND SPECIALTY STORE NOTES

_____

_____

_____

_____

_____

_____

_____

RECIPES

CRÈME FRAÎCHE

Crème fraîche is a wonderful and tasty substitute for boring sour cream, but it's relatively expensive to buy. Here is a super easy and much cheaper way to enjoy this delicacy:

2 T cultured buttermilk
1 c 40% (or heavy whipping) cream

- Stir buttermilk into heavy cream.
- Cover with cheesecloth, and let stand at room temperature, roughly 70°, for 10–24 hours, or until thick.
- At this point you can use it or refrigerate it for up to 10 days.

Crème fraîche makes a great base for flavors. Try adding vanilla if you are serving it with dessert, saffron if you are serving it with seafood, or fresh dill to go with your cucumber soup. Crème fraiche is hearty and will not curdle or break if added to pasta sauce or other hot items.

BEST CAULIFLOWER EVER (VEGAN) | SERVES 6

1 head cauliflower, chopped small
1 c walnuts, chopped
2 T olive oil, or your favorite flavored oil from one of the fine shops in this chapter
salt and pepper to taste

- Add the oil to a large sauté pan, and heat on high.
- Add cauliflower, and sauté until soft.
- When cauliflower begins to caramelize a bit, lower the heat to medium and add the walnuts.
- Sauté for about a minute more. If cooked too long, the walnuts will burn.
- Salt and pepper to taste.
- Serve to cauliflower skeptics and enthusiasts alike.

I serve this dish often and it serves me well. Over the years, I have turned many people on to this overlooked vegetable with this very recipe. This isn't the mushy, over salted cauliflower of the last generation. When I hear someone say, "I hate cauliflower," I know it's time to whip up a batch. It is great hot off the stove or cold out of the fridge.

BORSCHT (VEGAN) | SERVES 4–6

Though this recipe may turn your hands purple for a few minutes, it will warm your soul for much longer. I discovered borscht during the early days of Local Harvest Café when searching for delicious vegan soup options. It was an instant hit and remains a fixture on their soup menu. Serve it hot in the winter and cold in the summer—it is equally delicious both ways.

1 large onion, diced
2 T olive oil
4 large beets, peeled and cut into ½-inch cubes
4 carrots, peeled and chopped
1 large russet potato, peeled and cut into ½-inch cubes
3 T chopped fresh dill
½ c red wine vinegar (or the liquid from pickled beets, see p. 86)
1 c sour cream (optional garnish)
salt and pepper to taste

- Put olive oil and onions in soup pot, and sauté on medium heat until translucent.
- Add carrots and sauté another 5 minutes.
- Add beets and potatoes. Sauté a few more minutes.
- Add enough water or veggie stock to cover the vegetables.
- Gently boil until beets are soft.
- Add vinegar, dill, salt, and pepper.
- Serve warm or cold, and garnish with sour cream or créme fraîche if desired.

HEALTH FOODS

A health food store can be a wonderful labyrinth of interesting and hard to come by ingredients. As a rule their items are of high quality and, if you are lucky, they will have been produced using green or sustainable practices as well. The bulk of their inventory are the original "whole foods," packed with nutrients and lacking in additives or preservatives.

If you have any dietary restrictions (gluten-free, dairy-free, vegetarian, vegan, or allergies), pay regular visits to a health food emporium near you to stay abreast of new offerings and thinking. The employees at these stores often have an intimate knowledge of the products on the shelves and matters of health and nutrition—so don't hesitate to ask them about details.

There stores also devote huge sections to vitamins and supplements, and all-natural body care products.

INGREDIENTS AND PRODUCTS

EGG REPLACERS – used by vegans and others in place of eggs for baking.

FAIR TRADE PRODUCTS – products grown or manufactured in developing countries and traded to the U.S. under guidelines that ensure workers in those countries are fairly compensated for their work and are not otherwise exploited.

FLAXSEED – whole, meal, or oil; add to everyday foods for their Omega-3s. Great for pets, too.

GLUTEN-FREE PRODUCTS – products that don't include or have contact with wheat gluten.

GRAINS, ALL TYPES, BULK

- **brown rice** – a heartier and more nutritious choice than white rice.
- **bulgur** – cracked wheat; a great addition to salads and soups.
- **millet** – one of the world's oldest grains, low in flavor but high in protein. Bought dried and then boiled, millet provides a nice background for a bold dish such as curry or ratatouille.
- **oats** – yummy for a traditional breakfast. Use for making your own granola, and adding to cookies for additional fiber.
- **quinoa** – a nutty grain from Peru, bought dried and then boiled, quinoa is dense with vitamins and amino acids, and a staple in gluten-free diets.
- **spelt** – this ancient grain is native to southern Europe, full of vitamins and easy to digest. Its flour is frequently used as a replacement for wheat flour.

LOCAL PRODUCTS

MILKS, OTHER KINDS – essential for those not consuming dairy or soy, and a healthy way to spruce up your coffee or cereal. Usually in plain, vanilla, and chocolate.
- almond milk
- coconut milk
- hazelnut milk
- hemp milk
- rice milk

NATURAL PEANUT BUTTER – not the sugary stuff sold in most groceries, this is unadulterated crushed peanuts, sometimes with a bit of salt added.

NUT BUTTERS – great for kids and adults with peanut allergies, or just a good way to liven up your PB&J or smoothies.
- almond
- cashew
- macadamia
- soy
- sunflower

NUTS, ALL TYPES, BULK – raw, organic, roasted, unsalted, and other healthier preparations,

ORGANIC PRODUCTS – See p. 89 for more information.

SOY CHEESE – an alternative for those with lactose intolerance, or those watching calories.

SOY MILK – available in a range of flavors, sweetened or unsweetened.

SWEETENERS, ALTERNATIVE
- **agave** – a quick dissolving liquid with a low glycemic index, made from the same plant as tequila.
- **brown rice syrup** – a light-colored syrup, mild in sweetness and flavor, nice for cooking and baking.
- **honey** – unfiltered, flavored, and/or local, a favored sweetener since ancient times.
- **molasses** – a dark liquid with a sweet and earthy flavor, and more nutritious than most sweeteners.
- **stevia** – a sweetener derived from the stevia plant, handy for diabetics and those watching their sugar intake.

TEAS – green, herbal, and medicinal varieties.

TEMPEH – fermented soy bean cake, used like tofu.

TOFU – soybean cake, water-packed (in varying degrees of firmness), marinated, smoked, or deep fried.

VEGAN PRODUCTS – foodstuffs free of dairy, eggs, and all other animal by-products.

VITAMINS AND SUPPLEMENTS

INGREDIENTS AND PRODUCTS NOTES

_____

_____

_____

_____

_____

_____

_____

_____

STORES

DAYLIGHT NUTRITION
8565 Airport Rd.
Berkeley
314/522-8804

This shining spot in North St. Louis, where most of the grocery stores have been replaced by corner stores full of white bread and candy bars, Daylight Nutrition summons neighbors to skip the sugary sodas and fried chips in lieu of organic teas and unsalted roasted nuts. The smiling gentleman who runs the place is genuinely pleased for those who step through his doors and happy to be able to make a positive influence on his community.

This tiny but impressive store is stocked with all the healthy-life essentials: real juices, frozen vegetarian entrees, salad dressings, all natural sauces, flours, baking mixes, vitamins, homeopathic remedies, and supplements for common ailments like joint pain and diabetes, and detoxification. The ample bulk offerings include herbs, spices, and teas.

GOLDEN GROCER NATURAL FOODS
goldengrocer.com
335 N. Euclid Ave.
Central West End
314/367-0405

Golden Grocer Natural Foods is one of the original health food stores in St. Louis, opened during the mid-1970s when the Central West End first started its comeback. I remember going there as a child and, as an adult, I've been pleasantly surprised by its growth and its staying power.

May I say that this place is golden? Just take their bulk honey. It comes in five different flavors: tea tree, lavender, peppermint (can you imagine?!), almond, and plain. This honey is surrounded by a plethora of items sold in bulk—coffee, dried herbs (both for cooking and healing), dried fruits, grains, rice, pastas, beans, nuts, and even henna. It's an obvious and eco-friendly choice for stocking up on these basics.

For all those empty places in your cupboards, their grocery shelves are well-stocked with cereals and canned soups, vinegars and juices—the majority of it organic. Buy some flax seeds to add to your rice or smoothies, try all-natural beef or chicken broth in your next soup recipe, or replace that salty soy sauce with Bragg's Amino Acids, which have a similar flavor but more nutritive value.

Golden Grocer's produce is limited, but, after all, vitamins and supplements take up almost half the store. Find homeopathic medicines, curing teas, salves, vitamins, and minerals in at least five different brands. There are reference books to buy if you get a bit lost.

The entire front room of the store is dedicated to body care and well-being. Crammed with shampoos from herbal to castile, natural hair dyes, and essential body oils like lavender, rose, and calendula, it honestly makes me feel cleaner and shinier just standing in there. Don't just tend to your body's inner and outer health, sweeten your environment with 100% beeswax aromatherapy candles, incense, or a sage smudge stick.

This store is a St. Louis must-visit if you wish to live a healthier lifestyle and support a small local business.

LOCAL HARVEST GROCERY
localharvestgrocery.com
3148 Morganford Rd.
Tower Grove South
314/865-5260
See entry on p. 82.

THE NATURAL WAY HEALTH FOOD AND VITAMIN CENTERS
thenatway.com
8110 Big Bend Blvd.
Webster Groves
314/961-3541

12345 Olive Blvd.
Creve Coeur
314/878-3001

468 Old Smizer Mill Rd.
Fenton
636/343-4343

This local chain started in Webster in 1978, and has expanded from there. They opened a location in West County in 1990 and one in Fenton in 2000, responding to the demand for stores that promote health and well-being. Each store provides copiously towards that end, selling bulk grains, fair trade coffee and chocolate, and a full gamut of organic and all natural groceries.

Health food is not all tofu and granola here (though you can find that too). You can purchase things like organic grains and flours (e.g., Bob's Mill products), sprouted or gluten-free breads, bulk nuts and snacks, healthier chips and crackers, energy bars, vinegars, and treats like Rice Dream ice cream.

If you haven't tried chia seeds yet (same seeds that sprout into furry green Chia Pets!), pick up about two cups worth and try out the Chia Cherry "Rice" Pudding recipe on p. 75. It will amaze you. Or, swap that stale olive oil with increasingly popular (and heart-healthy, say some studies), very delicious coconut oil—the subtle coconut flavor will add an interesting layer to any dish. (If it's not solid at room temperature, it is not 100% coconut oil.) Don't forget to add briny, flaky sea salt to your pantry.

Natural Way carries a wonderful selection of natural body care products, including those from Burt's Bees. A large portion of each store is dedicated to vitamins, supplements, and natural healing, and one cool aspect of that is that they have their own Natural Way brand of vitamins and supplements. These are really affordable and made in the U.S.A.

NEW DAWN NATURAL FOODS
3536 Arsenal St.
South City
314/772-9110

Though a wee bit of a store, New Dawn Natural Foods is a one-stop-shop for vitamins, tinctures, herbs, and other natural remedies just off the South Grand Business District. You can also buy a smattering of natural beauty products, natural cleaning products, energy bars, pet food, books, soymilk, and sometimes produce here.

This is an easy place to make small, healthy changes. Grab some agave for your coffee (lower glycemic index) and give up sugar. Trade in whole milk for organic almond milk, which is creamy and generally considered more delicious than soy or rice milk. Instead of saturated fat, it's full of Omega-3s. After eating your last box of preservative-filled wheat crackers, stop here for crispy rice crackers made only of rice and a touch of oil.

I enjoy the personal feel of New Dawn. The shopkeepers are helpful and ready to order anything they don't have in stock, and the pretty little chocolates that taunt at the checkout always seem a worthy indulgence.

RIVER CITY NUTRITION
833 S. Kirkwood Rd.
Kirkwood
314/822-1406

River City Nutrition has the aura of a St. Louis institution. It's where you go to go vegan, eat gluten-free, or just add a few years to your life.

The large and spacious store has an old co-op feel to it, backed up with a supreme bulk foods section, showcasing grains, nuts, crackers, pasta, rice, and coffee. Wide grocery choices cover all kinds of energy bars and trail mixes, organic chips and cookies, nuts butters, and frozen all-natural entrees. In the refrigerators, they stock vegan butter, mayonnaise, cream cheese, and cheese substitutes. Many of their wares are organic, including cheese, butter, milk, bread, frozen veggies, and flours.

Look too for a large selection of vitamins, minerals, supplements, and books, and a small baby products area for new parents.

HEALTH FOOD STORE NOTES

_____

_____

_____

_____

_____

_____

_____

_____

RECIPES

CHOCOLATE APPLE UPSIDE DOWN CAKE (VEGAN) | SERVES 8

by Molly Brady

3–4 apples, peeled and sliced
½ c walnuts, chopped
1 c brown sugar
4 T vegan margarine or coconut oil
2 c soy milk
2 t apple cider vinegar
1¼ c sugar
⅔ c oil
2 t vanilla
2 c flour
⅔ c cocoa
1½ t baking soda
1 t baking powder
½ t salt
¾ c chocolate chips

- Preheat the oven to 350°.
- Use a tablespoon of the margarine to grease a 9" x 13" pan.
- Layer apples on the bottom of the pan.
- Add walnuts and brown sugar on top of apples.
- Dollop remaining margarine on top of the brown sugar.
- Combine soy milk and vinegar in a bowl. Set aside and allow to curdle for a few minutes.
- Add the sugar, oil, and vanilla to soy milk mixture. Beat until foamy.
- In a separate bowl, sift together dry ingredients.
- Add the dry ingredients in two batches to the wet ingredients and stir.
- Add chocolate chips.
- Mix only until no large lumps remain.
- Pour into pan and bake about 45 minutes, or until an inserted toothpick comes out clean.

CHERRY CHIA "RICE" PUDDING | SERVES 4

4 T raw chia seeds
2 c cow's milk or almond milk
¼ c dried cherries
½ t vanilla
1 dash cinnamon
1 t agave nectar

- Combine all ingredients, and mix well with a whisk or large spoon.
- Add more agave nectar, if desired, to increase sweetness.
- Allow the pudding to stand at least 30 minutes before serving, preferably in the fridge.
- Store in the refrigerator, and eat within a few days.

ROASTED VEGETABLES WITH WALNUTS AND QUINOA | SERVES 6

2 medium beets, peeled and diced
1 large sweet potato, peeled and diced
1 medium squash (butternut, acorn, or spaghetti), peeled and diced
3 red potatoes, diced
2 carrots, peeled and diced
3 cloves roasted garlic
3 c quinoa
6 c water
1 c toasted walnuts
salt and pepper to taste
vinaigrette or lemon juice to taste (optional)

Roast the vegetables.
- Pre-heat oven to 350°.
- Place diced vegetables (carrots, beets, sweet potato, red potatoes, and squash) on a baking tray, and roast until tender (about 45 minutes), stirring occasionally.

Toast the walnuts.
- While vegetables are roasting, toast walnuts by placing them on another a tray in the oven for 7 minutes.

Cook the quinoa.
• While the walnuts are toasting, start the quinoa.
• Place water, quinoa, and roasted garlic in sauce pan and bring to a boil.
• Reduce heat to simmer, and cover.
• Cook until water is absorbed (about 15 minutes). Do no stir while cooking.

Put it all together.
• Remove vegetables from the oven once tender.
• Place in a bowl, add quinoa and walnuts.
• Toss with salt and pepper.
• Serve immediately.
• Sometimes I like to top with vinaigrette or lemon juice for an added layer of flavor.

ROASTED EGGPLANT "MEATLOAF" | SERVES 8

6 medium sweet potatoes, roasted and skinned
4 eggplants, roasted and skinned
1½ c cooked bulgur
¼ c roasted garlic
½ yellow onion, diced and sautéed

2 T freshly ground flax seeds
2 T warm water

¼ c nutritional yeast
1 T black pepper
1 T cumin
2 T sage
2 T paprika
1 T thyme
1 T onion powder
1 T kosher salt
1 T soy sauce
3 T chili powder
1 T Dijon

1 c vital wheat gluten
1 c bread crumbs

- Preheat oven to 350°.
- Place first 5 ingredients into the bowl of a standup mixer. Using the paddle, beat the mixture till well mixed.
- Mix the ground flax seeds and warm water. Let stand until they get thick.
- Add flaxseed to the bowl along with all other ingredients except the wheat gluten and the bread crumbs.
- Mix until well incorporated.
- Add the final two ingredients, and mix well.
- Form mixture into a loaf on greased cookie sheet.
- Cover with tomato sauce, ketchup, or any delicious sauce.
- Bake until firm, about 45 minutes.
- Slice and serve warm.

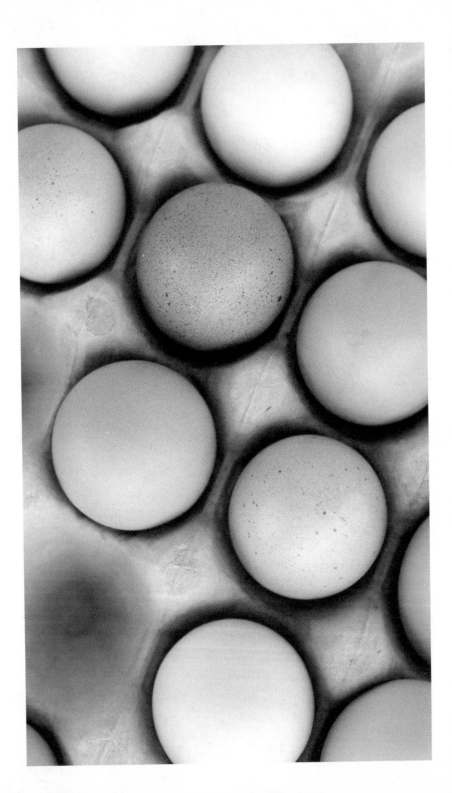

LOCAL PRODUCTS

The increase of interest in local products has arrived in St. Louis like a tidal wave (which, of course is not a local phenomenon at all!). Growing up I remember the only local produce you could find in most grocery stores were apples from Eckert's, the only local product was pasta sauce "made on The Hill," and the only local meat was from a factory farm in middle Missouri and available at the supermarket. "The little guy" existed back then, but in the corners and unknown places, patronized by a select few.

About ten years ago St. Louisans began to care *en masse* where their food was coming from and who was growing and producing it. Farmers markets have made a comeback, with over a dozen popping up, and a number of stores have opened to cater to the locally-minded customer. These markets and stores have in turn contributed to a resurgence in small businesses growing or producing local products. Small farmers and artisan producers have increased steadily in the last few years.

We now have at least two locally produced cleaning supply companies, an ever-popular potato chip producer, about five soap and beauty product companies, and dozens of small farms and ranches, all using organic and natural growing and raising methods. Then there are the many micro-coffee roasters, micro-breweries, and even micro-distilleries making some key beverages in our city. All these new small businesses have made it fun to shop again! They are constantly breaking the mold, trying new things, and challenging convention, not to mention providing us with extraordinary food, drink, and cleaning products.

This trend not only makes our shopping experiences more fulfilling and fun— it's also a needed and important boost to our local economy. It keeps money in the area and pays farmers and producers a real living wage as they can sell their fruits, vegetables, meat, and other wares close to home. I have included a handful of places where you'll find a large amount of local products, but these are not the only places. Keep your eyes out at every store you go into. Go out and support our neighbors!

To support farmers directly, head to your local farmers market (there's a whole separate chapter, *Farmers Markets and Seasonal Produce*, see p. 98) or sign up for a CSA (Community Supported Agriculture) subscription (see p. 90).

FAVORITE LOCAL PRODUCTS

_____

_____

_____

_____

_____

_____

_____

STORES

LADUE MARKET
9155 Clayton Rd.
Ladue
314/993-0184

This quirky little market can be easy to miss, especially in the winter when their normal crush of potted plants isn't out front. Opened in 1928, Ladue Market is housed in a plain building with very little signage along a very busy stretch of Clayton Road. They must like it that way because even with these impediments the market appears to be thriving.

This place makes me feel like I'm in Manhattan—it's very small, but uses the space wisely. Case in point: They stock probably about half of their one hundred wines above the refrigeration case, the liquor is stashed above the produce, and the beer is randomly placed throughout the store.

The packaged selections here may range from high to average quality (e.g., coffee ranges from Illy to Folgers), but the produce is fresh and bountiful. You can find all the fruit and veggie staples, as well as "gourmet" vegetables like fingerling potatoes, white asparagus, and purple broccoli. This family-owned store has been buying produce and meat directly from farmers since they opened almost ninety years ago, and they aren't planning on stopping anytime soon. Don't forget to grab some orange juice squeezed right in the store.

Their deli/meat counter is small, but again, looks are deceiving. The case itself is full of Boar's Head deli meat and miscellaneous cheeses for slicing, a mix of seafood (crab claws, salmon, tuna, shrimp, tilapia, oysters), and the usual cuts of beef, chicken, and pork. It doesn't stop there, because they stock more behind the counter. If you don't see it, just ask. Plus, they take special orders and can cut almost anything. Some of their fresh pork, beef, and chicken come from small Missouri farms—they don't advertise it, so again, just ask. They're happy to talk to you about the origin of all their meats.

Ladue Market also carries prepared meals, great artisan cheeses, fresh loaves of Companion bread, and interesting mixers for their liquors. Yes, one amazing little market.

LOCAL HARVEST GROCERY
localharvestgrocery.com
3148 Morganford Rd.
Tower Grove South
314/865-5260

So, you'd like to ride the "Local Food" train? This is it. This independent grocery shines through the dullness of most full-service grocers. You can still find ground beef just like at any other store, but the checker here can tell you the name of the farmer/s and how their cows are raised. Pick up a bag of apples and you'll hear a story about the origin of the farmers' trees and how they're fertilized with fish waste from a nearby tilapia farm. Fill your cart with soap and laundry detergent, and the person in front of you at the checkout just might be the person who made it.

Local Harvest focuses on selling locally grown fruits and vegetables as well as locally made foods and home products, hitting and usually surpassing their goal of stocking fifty percent local products from nearby farms, small businesses, and start-ups. The shelves are full of local gems, like Stinger honey from Kirkwood, Goshen Coffee from Edwardsville, and Billy Goat Potato Chips and Better Life cleaning products from St. Louis. Other local products include frozen pizza, ice cream, soup mixes, chocolates, and lip balms.

This is a grocery store with a conscience, no doubt. The owners of Local Harvest pay close attention to how the food they sell is produced, what goes into premade items, and the type of packaging it comes in. You can feel virtually guilt-free when shopping here, knowing that they've already considered the Earth and the community for you.

If you are plagued with allergies, dietary restrictions, or the like, this is also the place to find gluten-free, vegan, and other allergy friendly products. The staff is super well-educated and respectful of all types of diets. You may even learn a thing or two…

The local produce is really the high point of this store, and most of it comes from the farmers with stands at the farmers markets in the area. In the summer, close to seventy-five percent of the fruits and veggies sold are produced in the area (that amount naturally drops in the winter months). The meat freezer is not-to-be-missed, as it is chockfull of free-range chicken, pork, lamb, bison, and grass-fed beef from Missouri and Illinois.

Local Harvest also sells beer (local) and wine (local and non-local), and even a few local artisan non-food crafts (like beeswax candles and hand-made cards).

The store has a café too. It's across the street and produces the prepared foods stocked in the refrigerator cases of the store. Look for house-made hummus, ready-to-bake entrees, and various soups. They also offer full-service catering for just about any type of event.

MAUDE'S MARKET
maudesmarket.com
4219 Virginia Ave.
South City
314/353-4219

Maude's Market popped up a few years ago to relieve an area considered to be a "food desert," a neighborhood stranded with little access to fresh and healthy food. This six-hundred-square-foot store (yeah, that's pretty small) boosts a whole lot of local food, from the carrots to the coffee to the eggs. The owner, a former grass-roots political organizer in D.C., came to Dutchtown to open this quaint market in 2010. Since then, the cute pocket-sized storefront has been abuzz with energy from the new wave of popularity for local and seasonal foods.

The most popular things on the shelves include free range eggs, Stringbean Coffee (St. Louis's newest micro-roaster), pasture raised meatballs from Circle B Ranch in the Ozark Hills, certified organic Elixir Farms beef, and local pecans and honey.

Recently, Maude's started a CSA program that is both easy and affordable. You can renew monthly (one pickup a month) or simply seasonally (roughly ten weeks) for just $35 per week for a single share, which includes meat, produce, and grains. You can get your CSA vegetarian, pescatarian, gluten-free, pork free, and paleo.

Take a few minutes to explore and cherish this addition to the St. Louis food scene…local pasture raised meat and fish in the freezer; piles of locally grown produce; shelves of small-batch honey, coffee, and soaps; fresh locally-made pasta; and organic Illinois yogurt. You can grab a Geisert Farms pork chop, make a sauce with Sandhill Farm mustard, cook up some local greens, and make a honey crème brulée for dessert (with pasture raised eggs, of course).

PARKER'S TABLE
parkerstable.com
7118 Oakland Ave
Clayton
314/645-2050
See p. 56.

WINSLOW'S HOME AND FARM
7213 Delmar Blvd.
University City
314/725-7559

Winslow's is an "urban general store" in University City, gracing Delmar with yet another cool place to shop. Let me say—this place has a little bit of everything. From tools and umbrellas to greeting cards and flowers, it really is a general store, complete with groceries of good quality and an amazing café in the back. The middle section of the store functions as a dining room sprinkled with tools (and not just cooking tools), gardening equipment, greeting cards, and small gifts, like artisan soaps, blank journals, cute knickknacks, and tons of retro-style toys (where's the last place you saw Tiddlywinks?).

The back half of the store has a row of glass-front refrigeration, housing beautiful produce, along with dairy products and prepared foods made in house. About seventy-five percent of their produce is local (when the season is right), and half of that comes from their own farm near Augusta, Missouri, where they also produce eggs and fresh herbs. All the meat they sell, and ninety percent of the meat they use, is local.

Tucked in the back corner is their little counter, where they serve breakfast, brunch, lunch, and early dinner. You can just walk up to the counter and order any number of scrumptious items and sit at one of their charming tables, inside or out. Be sure to top off your meal with a locally roasted coffee.

The rest of the store is dedicated to wine and beer, the selection of the former being much larger.

LOCAL PRODUCTS STORE NOTES

_____

_____

_____

_____

RECIPES

PASTA E FAGIOLI | SERVES 6

1 lb. (2½ c) dried navy or cannellini beans, uncooked
1 medium onion, halved
10 cloves of garlic, just smashed once with the side of the knife
8 fresh sage leaves
¾ c extra virgin olive oil

2 lbs fresh St. Louis made pasta (see below)
1 small can whole peeled tomatoes, chopped
4 cloves garlic, minced
salt and freshly ground black pepper
freshly grated parmesan

- Place beans in a heavy pot with enough water to cover.
- Bring water to a boil, then strain beans and return to pot.
- Add fresh water to cover.
- Add onion halves, garlic, 6 of the sage leaves, and ½ cup of the olive oil.
- Cover and bring to a boil.
- Reduce heat to low, and simmer until beans are tender, about 45 minutes.
- Strain beans. Transfer beans to a mixing bowl.
- Chop remaining 2 sage leaves and stir into beans, along with remaining ¼ cup olive oil.
- Boil water for pasta. Cook until al dente.
- Add pasta, tomatoes, garlic, salt, and pepper to beans in bowl, and toss.
- Top with freshly grated parmesan.

ARTISAN PASTA IN ST. LOUIS

Almost every foodie has had their turn making pasta in their home. Some have actually succeeded. Now that the pasta roller is in the pantry collecting dust, leave it right where it's at. Step out and find some locally made fresh pasta instead.

At the turn of the century, St. Louis had at least ten pasta manufacturers, making use of "Missouri's location, in the heart of the wheat-filled plains," Patricia Corrigan explains in her book *Eating St. Louis: The Gateway City's Unique Food Culture* (St. Louis University, 2008). Today, that number has dwindled to two. Midwest Pasta (formerly known as Mangia Italiano) and Stellina Pasta, both located in South City, are the last holdouts of the lost art of fresh pasta making.

Midwest Pasta's original incarnation, Mangia Italiano, opened almost thirty years ago as a small Italian market. The owner, Doc Parmely, invested in finely crafted pasta making machines from Italy and began the job of teaching himself to make pasta. Over the years, the storefront at 3145 S. Grand Boulevard went through many changes and now is a restaurant and bar bearing the same name. But they still make pasta the same way Doc did, even with some of his machines in their new location on Cherokee Street, bearing the name Midwest Pasta.

Starting with durum and semolina flours (freshly ground at a mill on South Broadway), they add cracked eggs (freshly laid on the other side of the Mississippi River), filtered water, and sometimes wonderful flavoring agents to concoct pastas of just about every shape (radiatore), conchiglie, fettucini, spaghetti, linguini), color (even purple, black, and bright green), and flavor (squid ink, beet, spinach, tomato, whole wheat). The pasta is worked in small batches using old world techniques that result in a superb product.

Find Midwest Pasta in the refrigerated section of Winslow's Home (see p. 84), Local Harvest Grocery (see p. 82), and Whole Foods (see p. 139). It's served by close to thirty restaurants in the area.

Stellina is considerably younger, but they too have a definite grasp on pasta making. Stellina Pasta founder, Jamey Tochtrop, has been making pasta by hand for about ten years. Mostly self-taught, Jamey works with stand mixers to mix the pasta dough, but he also kneads it by hand before rolling it out to the desired shape. He imported the machine he uses to roll out and cut the pasta dough from Italy. He uses 100% organic grains milled in Kansas and beautiful brown-shell eggs. Featured Stellina pasta flavors include whole wheat, flax seed, herb, and whole wheat walnut.

The pride of Jamey's pasta making is his handmade agnolotti, stuffed with all kinds of delicious and fresh fillings. These fresh pastas can be purchased, or eaten, at Stellina, a South City restaurant (3342 Watson Rd).

PICKLED BEETS

Pickling beets ain't that hard.

When fall sneaks up on you, it's the time to savor the last bits of summer and look forward to the root vegetables to come. Beets are one of my favorites. They're hearty, delicious, and oh-so-good for you. With so many varieties to choose from—red, golden, white, and even striped—beets create a lovely color palette in any dish.

As a kid, I never liked pickled beets, but I think that is because I never had *real* pickled beets. One evening, a couple of years ago, I walked into my friend Katie's kitchen and was immediately hit by the smell of vinegar and the sight of deep red, freshly pickled beets. I stared at the huge glass jar and wondered what kind of magic it was.

She explained the process to me, something I never learned in culinary school, and I knew I had to do it myself. And I did, with fantastic results.

You should too. It's really easy.

5 large beets, from your closest farmers market
½ c sugar or ¼ c St. Louis made honey
1 c white or cider vinegar (cider is tastier)
½ c water
3 T pickling spice
½ t salt
1 T whole black peppercorns

- Scrub the beets and remove the greens, but don't pierce the skin.
- Boil the beets until the flesh is tender, that's when you can put a fork in with little resistance.
- Drain and cool slightly.
- While beets are cooling, mix all other ingredients in a pot.
- Heat ingredients until salt and sugar are melted and you see a few bubbles.
- Peel and slice beets, and fill a glass jar or jars with them.
- Pour hot liquid over beets.
- Serve immediately, or place lid on jar, refrigerate, and enjoy later.
- Bonus: These will last in the fridge for about two months.

Sometimes I like to add carrots, onions, or turnips to the beets. Yum!

See, it ain't that hard. And just so you know, beets contain fiber, iron, calcium, phosphorus, niacin, vitamins A and C, and small amounts of protein.

PRODUCE

There is something exciting happening in St. Louis: fresh local produce is becoming more commonly available. We have no less than a dozen large farmers markets in the metro area and even grocery stores are beginning stock more of the beautiful variety of local fruits and veggies that Missouri has to offer as one of the top agricultural states in the union.

As our society speeds up, and people begin to take more meals on the go, it is wonderful to see farmers holding onto the most important traditions of growing food. There is nothing more soul satisfying than piles of brightly colored vegetables, bunches of pungent herbs, and pints of glistening berries. I have included a seasonal vegetable and fruit calendar for this part of the country in the *Farmers Market and Seasonal Produce* chapter that comes right after this one on p. 98. Use it for meal planning and menu writing—and for getting super excited about what might show up at the markets in the next month.

Missouri boasts the second largest number of farmers working in a state in the U.S. This bounty of local farmers pushes each one to grow specialized varieties of produce to stay competitive. Our Missouri farmers grow any number of types of squash (globe, patty pan, delicata), tomatoes (purple Cherokee, zebra, sun gold), greens (mizuna, sorrel, tatsoi), potatoes (Peruvian blue, fingerling, Viking red), eggplant (white, Japanese), and herbs (lemon thyme, catmint, savory), to name but a smattering of what's available. Many producers are also finding that the popularity of shopping and eating local allows them to grow staples like yellow onions, carrots, and red potatoes in a more cost-effective way.

Community supported agriculture (CSA) is another way to procure fresh and local produce. CSA is a farmer, or group of farmers, who sell subscriptions by the growing season and, though they all differ, most deliver a basket of seasonal produce once a week to a pick-up site near your home. The main mantra for CSAs is "share the risk, share the reward"—meaning you pay for the subscription at the beginning of the growing season, and your share is as big as nature allows. This is a great way to save time and to support your farmers directly. If you find the share you receive too large, consider sharing the cost and the food with a neighbor. These programs give money directly to the farmers and help the farmers make a living wage.

WHAT IS ORGANIC?

Everyone is familiar with organic food, right? I mean, even Walmart has its own organic line these days. Everyone knows that organic is better for you, right? But how many of us actually know what organic means and why it's better for us?

The official national guidelines for acquiring organic certification were set by the USDA in 2000 and state that produce must be grown under certain conditions:

- No use of artificial fertilizers, chemical/conventional pesticides, or sewer sludge (i.e., human waste).
- Mandatory use of organically produced seeds and planting stock.
- Mandatory rotation of crops to retain soil nutrients.
- Permitted use of approved chemicals from a very short list.
- No use of genetically modified seeds or plant stock.
- No exposure to irradiation nor any additives allowed.
- Mandatory use of sustainable growing practices (i.e., practices that allow the natural ecosystem to thrive).
- All conditions for growing must be recorded in detailed logs.

In turn, these guidelines produce a healthier and tastier product. Without chemical intervention, the produce can grow under its natural conditions and ends up containing more vitamins and antioxidants. This also limits toxins in the bodies of those who eat it and toxins in the land that grows it (and the run-off). Sustainable farming practices are better for the environment and generally use less fossil fuels.

Organic is, not surprisingly, usually more expensive, but there is much more to gain by eating it.

A SHORT EXPLANATION OF ORGANIC LABELING:

- **100% organic** – grown and/or produced under USDA organic guidelines.

- **organic** – 95% of the product has been grown and/or produced under USDA organic guidelines.

- **made with organic ingredients** – at least 70% of the product has been grown and/or produced using the USDA organic guidelines, and the remaining 30% has not been genetically engineered, irradiated, or fertilized with sewer sludge.

CSAs

DRY DOCK FARM
riverhillspoultry.com
Silex, MO
573/384-5859

Known for their gorgeous cage-free eggs, Dry Dock Farm offers a twenty-two-week CSA of wonderful variety that includes eight different vegetables, a seasonal fruit, herbs, and a dozen of their delicious eggs every week. Using all natural, bio-intensive growing methods, Dry Dock produces safe and natural products for your dinner table. One option will deliver these goods straight to your door every week. Another delivers them to a group pickup site for a little bit of a discount.

Apart from vegetables and eggs, for a little extra this CSA subscription will include products from their fellow members of the River Hills Poultry Alliance. The alliance is a project based in Northeast Missouri that brings together small-scale heritage egg producers, who support each other with information and equipment. Dry Dock uses these relationships to make crafts and products from their partners—things like antibiotic-free pork, humanely raised chickens, goat cheese, jams, pickles, and raw honey—available to their subscribers.

Something really special Dry Dock offers is a winter share, delivered every other week in November and December. This is separate from their normal season and includes winter vegetables like potatoes, turnips, hearty greens, and carrots, as well as eggs and great products from their River Hills Poultry Alliance partners.

Husband-and-wife team Mark and Michelle both come from passionate, food-loving families and bought this farm in 2005. They have since included their sons and daughters in this venture to make it a real family-run farm.

FAIR SHARES
fairshares.org
St. Louis

Fair Shares, run by sister duo Sara and Jamie, is not connected to any one farm. Aiming to make a year round CSA that is more than just produce, these ladies began distributing locally produced goods and some produce from a variety of purveyors for their members in 2007. This CSA is based on an annual subscription, which means you get food all year round and are not constrained to a growing season as with most CSAs. Best of all, Fair Shares offers more than just vegetables. Subscribers receive local meat, handcrafted pasta, fresh breads, hormone-free dairy, and cage-free eggs.

They offer pickup at three sites (South City, University City, and Kirkwood). Having over 450 members allows them to schedule a range of pickup options, meaning you can most likely pick the best time and location for you. Fair Shares, with the help of a mostly volunteer staff, has doubled in size since its beginning in 2008, and has single-handedly helped many small St. Louis producers grow their businesses by signing up committed customers for regular shares of their products. How invaluable for small start-ups with perishable products!

Good for them, but better for you: Imagine, for about $50 a week, you can support your small local farmers and producers without ever having to step foot in a crowded farmers market or grocery store.

MAUDE'S MARKET
maudesmarket.com
4219 Virginia Ave.
Dutchtown
314/353-4219
See entry on p. 83.

THREE RIVERS COMMUNITY FARM
threeriverscommunityfarm.com
Elsah, IL
618/374-9470

This farm offers a twenty-six-week subscription, from mid-May to November, and a customizable 13-week version too. They offer chemical-free produce from their small farm in Elsah, over the border in Illinois.

Three Rivers has five pickup sites around town—University City, Maplewood, Maplewood Farmers Market, Tower Grove Farmers' Market, and at the farm itself. Choose the farm and you get to see how it all happens. These shares permit use of the twelve-acre farm for recreational purposes. Go for a picnic, nap, stroll, or pick-your-own possibilities.

Expect such things as fresh salad mix, herbs, scallions, beets, summer squash, heirloom tomatoes, carrots, and eggplants on your table half the year, all grown free of chemical fertilizers, pesticides, and herbicides. For a small upcharge, you can also add their humanely raised eggs to your subscription.

WEEKLY HARVEST FROM LOCAL HARVEST GROCERY
localharvestgrocery.com
South City and Kirkwood
314/865-5260 or 314/966-6566

Local Harvest Grocery started in a six-hundred-square-foot storefront in South City in 2008. Owners Maddie and Pat wanted nothing more than to offer local food to people year round. Only a few years later, they are doing that and more. Now with bigger stores and over $1 million paid to local producers, LHG offers a CSA pick-up at both grocery locations once a week. These seasonally themed shares deliver lovely local meat, produce, dry goods, cheese, coffee, and specialty products from producers in a 150-mile radius. Weekly Harvest is available year round, your choice of vegetarian, omnivore, or paleo.

These shares are not simply picked from the grocery's shelves—the good people that put together the Weekly Harvest boxes create their own relationships with producers and often get products that can't be found in the store. Weekly Harvesters' weekly commitment to local stuff gets them first crack at new and exciting produce, cheese, and specialty items.

Each box can feed two people for a week without much other grocery shopping required! They're thinking about offering delivery soon, but picking up your share gives you the opportunity to browse the packed shelves of this local treasure, a glorious combination of grocery, health food store, and specialty boutique (see p. 82 for full description).

YELLOWTREE FARM
yellowtreefarm.com
Fenton

Justin Lesczc, the owner of YellowTree Farm, is one of the most colorful characters in the cast of new boutique farmers. Whether it's putting free range chicken fat in the lip balm he sells or adding fresh bamboo shoots to your favorite restaurant's menu—Justin is sure to surprise. He's the kind of guy who would show up at my restaurant's back door, spouting facts about the deliciousness and nutritional values of some wild foraged edibles or a new variety of potato. The idiosyncrasies of his passion are a good thing. If a Yellow TreeFarm share is anything like the owner, expect it to be interesting, surprising, charming, and in good taste. The produce and foraged edibles of this farm have always been of great quality. Along with produce, the subscription includes corn and wheat grown by the farm and milled by a neighbor.

CSA NOTES

_____

_____

_____

_____

_____

_____

_____

_____

STORES

FARMERS MARKETS
See entry on p. 100.

LOCAL HARVEST GROCERY
localharvetgrocery.com
3148 Morganford Rd.
Tower Grove South
314/865-5260
See entry on p. 82.

ROGER'S PRODUCE
625 E. Lockwood Ave.
Webster Groves
314/962-9157

This old roadside produce stand holds a sweet place in my heart, as my family shopped here when I was growing up. Vivid memories still stick with me—the smell of the brown bags my mother used to fill with fresh vegetables, the boxes of crisp apples at ground level (perfect kid height), and how Mom always grabbed a little bag of roasted peanuts for my father just before checking out.

The building that has housed Roger's Produce for the past thirty years was originally a gas station, and brings to mind the time when Webster Groves was just a burgeoning farming community. With all the big wooden crates and bushel baskets, the feel of a vintage farmstand prevails. The very front of the stand is usually covered in the season's best, like colorful sunny bedding plants in the spring and bright pumpkins in October. Under the open-air roof is box after box of just about any mainstream produce you could want, from potatoes to onions to broccoli to bananas, all relatively inexpensive. Roger's sells about 26 to 35 percent local produce.

After filling the small brown bags with your favorite beans or mushrooms, go inside the tiny building to have your vegetables weighed. I am happy to report the bins of roasted peanuts are still there.

When I last asked the man behind the counter when they close for the winter, he sort of rolled his eyes and smiled: "Believe it or not, we are open all year round. Everyone thinks we are closed in the winter, but we are here."

PRODUCE STORE NOTES

_____
_____
_____
_____
_____
_____
_____
_____

RECIPES

ASPARAGUS MILANESE | SERVES 4

20 spears asparagus
4 farm fresh eggs
2 T oil
parmesan for grating

- Put one tablespoon of oil in a large sauté pan, and heat to medium heat.
- Add the asparagus.
- Cook until bright green and soft, about one minute.
- Distribute spears across four plates.
- Add the other tablespoon of oil to the pan. Heat again to medium heat.
- Crack the eggs into the pan, and cook until the whites are firm.
- Place one egg on each plate, directly over the asparagus.
- Grate parmesan on top of egg. Serve immediately.

SHAVED BRUSSELS SPROUTS | SERVES 4

Four words of introduction: best brussels sprouts ever.

½ lb brussels sprouts, shaved
1 T olive oil
1 c walnuts, chopped
salt and pepper to taste

- Place shaved brussels into a large skillet. Add salt and pepper.
- Cook on high heat till slightly caramelized.
- Add walnuts, and cook for a few more minutes.
- Serve and enjoy.

KOHLRABI GRATIN | SERVES 2

This underserved and underappreciated vegetable is actually super delicious.

2 small heads of kohlrabi, cleaned, with greens removed and set aside, peeled and sliced into thin rounds
½ c grated parmesan or other hard cheese
½ c heavy cream
½ T butter
fresh cracked pepper

Note: *This recipe can be doubled or tripled and made in a larger container.*

- Preheat oven to 400°.
- Butter two 8-oz oven-safe ramekins.
- Alternate layers of kohlrabi and cheese in each ramekin until you reach the top.
- Heat cream and butter until warm. Pour half into each ramekin.
- Top with cheese and fresh cracked pepper.
- Bake for 45 to 55 minutes.
- Sauté kohlrabi greens.
- Serve warm greens on top of gratin, or as a side.

GARLICKY GREENS

5–7 cloves garlic, peeled, sliced
enough olive oil to cover the bottom of a wide sauté pan
big handfuls of greens (baby mustard, turnip, chard), stems pulled off and discarded, and roughly shredded
salt and freshly ground black pepper

- Place sauté pan over medium heat.
- When the pan is hot, add just enough oil to cover the bottom of the pan.
- Add the garlic, stirring constantly
- Once the slivers turn golden, add the greens and toss to coat with the hot oil.
- Season with salt and pepper as soon as the greens start to wilt, and plate immediately.
- Turbocharge the garlic: Finely mince another clove of garlic, and add to the greens during the final 30 seconds of cooking. Toss the greens to distribute, keeping the pan and the greens moving constantly, if you can.
- Serve as a side dish, or toss with pasta and serve as a main course.

FARMERS MARKETS AND SEASONAL PRODUCE

Farmers markets have emerged as an energetic hub of the food community in this town, a place where anyone can buy their food straight from the source, sometimes even shaking the same hand that harvested your heirloom tomatoes or biodynamic purple carrots.

These markets provide shoppers with a healthy sense of community, an opportunity to know where their food is coming from, and a diverse selection of products that are as fresh as possible, not to mention the opportunity to return to real person-to-person connection with the circumstances surrounding our food, adding greater depth to our eating experience. These relationships give farmers a voice, allow them to reach customers directly, and restore for them some role as civic leaders.

At another level, shopping at the farmers market is an investment in your neighbors and your region as it puts money back into local businesses and farms. The thriving of farmers markets in St. Louis is strengthening our state's rural communities and displacing their dependency on corporate farming techniques and associations.

SEASONAL PRODUCE

MISSOURI AND ILLINOIS PRODUCE MONTH BY MONTH

Below is a very rough estimate of when certain produce is available in our region, subject to Mother Nature's whims or the existence of a greenhouse. Remember, food in season always tastes better.

APRIL – asparagus, lettuce, spinach

EARLY MAY – asparagus, chard, lettuce, radishes, spinach

LATE MAY – asparagus, lettuce, peas, rhubarb, spinach, strawberries

EARLY JUNE – asparagus, cabbage, lettuce, peas, radishes, raspberries, rhubarb, spinach

LATE JUNE – beets, blackberries, cabbage, carrots, peas, raspberries, rhubarb

EARLY JULY – beets, blackberries, carrots, corn, cucumbers, eggplant, green beans, okra, peaches, peas, peppers, potatoes, squash, tomatoes, watermelon

LATE JULY AND AUGUST – blackberries, cantaloupe, corn, cucumbers, eggplant, green beans, nectarines, okra, peaches, peas, peppers, plums, potatoes, squash, tomatoes, watermelon

SEPTEMBER – apples, beets, cucumbers, eggplant, green beans, lettuce, peaches, peas, peppers, potatoes, raspberries, squash, tomatoes, watermelon winter squash

EARLY OCTOBER – apples, beets, broccoli, brussels sprouts, cabbage, carrots, eggplant, peppers, potatoes, pumpkins, radishes, raspberries, spinach, sweet potatoes, tomatoes, winter squash

LATE OCTOBER – apples, beets, broccoli, brussels sprouts, cabbage, cauliflower, potatoes, spinach, sweet potatoes, winter squash

NOVEMBER – broccoli, brussels sprouts, cabbage, cauliflower, spinach, sweet potatoes, winter squash

SEASONAL PRODUCE NOTES

_____

_____

_____

_____

_____

FARMERS MARKETS

Because of the seasonal nature of Farmers Markets, as well as how they have been popping up like dandelions, I have not had the chance to go to every market in this book. I have supplied extra description for the markets with which I am most familiar, but I will be updating farmers market information on our website ShopLikeAChef.com frequently in the coming year.

ARNOLD FARMERS MARKET
745 Jeffco Blvd.
Arnold
Saturdays, May–October, 8 a.m.–Noon

CARONDELET FARMERS' MARKET
carondeletfarmersmarket.wordpress.com
7701 S. Broadway
Carondelet
Saturdays, June–October, 7 a.m.–Noon

CLAYTON FARMER'S MARKET
claytonfarmersmarket.com
8282 Forsyth Blvd.
Clayton
Saturdays, late May–late October, 8:30 a.m.–12:30 p.m.

The Clayton Farmer's Market is one of the higher quality, more expensive markets in town.

This is a medium-sized market, with a variety of foods. (For what you can't find, just go next door to Straub's.) With its fifteen to twenty vendors, including places like Biver Farms, Silent Oaks Farm, and Double Star Farms, you can buy tons of beautiful local produce here. And more than produce. There are artisan foods like goat cheese from Baetje Farms, fresh bread from Black Bear Bakery, pasture raised lamb from Prairie Grass Farm, and honey from Joy Stinger; handmade soaps; starter plants in the spring; and gourds in the fall. You can even line up for Blues Hog BarbeQue for lunch.

Or, just roam around for inspiration.

Look for special events like a pie baking contest, an Iron Chef Competition, and musical acts.

FERGUSON FARMERS MARKET
fergusonfarmersmarket.com
20 S. Florissant Rd.
Ferguson
314/524-1820
Saturdays, April–November, 8 a.m.–Noon

This North County market has twenty to thirty vendors, about a third of which are local artisans showing off their crafts. Women will be making beads, knitting scarves, weaving baskets, and sewing blankets at their booths while the market is underway. There are also soaps, candles, dried flowers, and jewelry.

The remaining vendors—the farmers—are selling locally grown produce, farm-fresh eggs, nuts, honey, spices, fresh-cut flowers, mustards, jams, cookies, Amish pasta, and dried beans. A few vendors carry Missouri beef, pork, chicken, sausage, and jerky.

Special events include chef demonstrations, food contests, featured local artists, bike rides twice each month, and special activities for children. There's weekly live music, too, better enjoyed with some freshly purchased produce, fresh baked breads, a freshly cooked omelette, or some sticky cotton candy.

KIRKWOOD FARMERS' MARKET
downtownkirkwood.com/farmers'-market.aspx
150 E. Argonne Dr.
Kirkwood
Mondays–Fridays, 9 a.m.–6 p.m.
Saturdays, 8 a.m.–5 p.m.
Sunday hours vary by vendor
April–October, limited hours for Thanksgiving and Christmas

This "farmers market" is a "Kirkwood Tradition" that occurs right in the middle of downtown Kirkwood. Unlike a classic farm market or the more recent boutique farmers markets, you can find more than just produce or locally produced products here. Expect to find all types of produce (shipped in from all over the country) side by side with Amish jam, little plastic toys, and candy. Still, along with the brokers (vendors who sell produce they don't personally grow), you will be able to buy local veggies, eggs, and cheese from local vendors.

At Christmastime, vendors will have decorative tins of nuts or cookies for sale, at Halloween there will be loads of cookies decorated as ghosts or witches, and at Easter their booths are piled high with festive plastic eggs and pastel colored baskets. These folks are ready for every holiday so you can be too.

Special events include a Peach Festival, pet themed days, a pumpkin patch, and local music.

MAPLEWOOD FARMERS MARKET
schlafly.com/bottleworks/farmers-market
Schlafly Bottleworks
7260 Southwest Ave.
Maplewood
Wednesdays, May–October, 4 p.m.–7 p.m.

This market started very small, but has morphed into to a middle-of-the-week institution for many. For those who can't make it to a market on Saturday, or are just plain out of delicious produce by Wednesday, this little gem is tailor made for you.

You can usually find (in season, of course) perky greens, ripe tomatoes, and plant starters. On top of that, there are favorites like baked goods (savory and sweet) from Black Bear or Four Seasons, pork and beef from Hinkebein, lamb and eggs from Prairie Grass Farms, jams from Centennial Farms, and produce from Claverach, Root Cellar, Biver Farms, and many more.

When you're done shopping, step inside the Schafly Bottleworks microbrewery for a freshly brewed, delicious beer.

NORTH CITY FARMERS' MARKET
northcityfarmersmarket.blogspot.com
St. Louis Ave. and N. 14th St., in front of Crown Candy Kitchen
Saturdays, June–October, 9 a.m.–Noon

OVERLAND FARMERS MARKET
overlandfarmersmarket.com
Overland Market Center
2500 block of Warson
Saturdays, May–October, 8 a.m.–12:30 p.m.

SOULARD FARMERS MARKET
www.soulardmarket.com
730 Carroll St.
Downtown
314/622-4180
Wednesdays, Thursdays, Fridays, year round, 8 a.m. –5 p.m.
Saturdays, year round, 6 a.m. –5 p.m.

Soulard has been a great staple of our fair city since 1779, earning it bragging rights as the oldest in the Midwest. What it has lost in horse-and-buggy charm over the years, it makes up for in its hugeness and bustle. There is history seeping from its pores and rafters.

This market is comprised of a small building—called "The Grand Hall"—and four covered outdoor wings. Each wing is crammed full of vendors selling everything from shoes to onions to puppies. Even if you don't buy anything the people watching is unbeatable—a real taste of St. Louis.

The guidelines to participate in the farmers market component of Soulard are pretty lenient. Many of the produce vendors are brokers, which means they buy produce from other places (mostly large produce vendors at Produce Row on Broadway) and resell it at their booths. Though this produce doesn't come from a local farm, it is much cheaper than their equivalents at conventional grocery stores. A few local farms do sell their handpicked produce, however, and some local artisans are represented, offering their handmade cheeses, soaps, balms, and whatnot for sale.

Though the vendors change frequently, a few stalwarts remain year after year:

BLACK BEAR BAKERY – an all organic, natural, and fully worker-owned bakery.

CHEESY JOHN – delicious and affordable cheeses.

KRUSE GARDENS – a local farmer with lots of boutique and heirloom varieties.

PET AND FEED SHOP – pets galore and the products they require and desire.

SAL'S – mid-range quality produce, but he and his daughters are almost always willing to strike a deal—so don't be shy.

SCHARF FARM – a great local farm with tons of beautiful produce and apples.

SEIBERT MEATS – local meats, fish, eggs, bacon, and fresh beans.

SOULARD BAKERY – classic baked goods

SOULARD FLORIST – with their giant selection of flowers.

SOULARD SPICE SHOP – see p. 117.

Wednesdays and Thursdays are relatively light days with only about half the vendors that are there on weekends. Friday is a little livelier. I enjoy it best because it's not too crowded and I can talk to the farmers. Saturday has the most vendors and the most customers.

Think about Saturdays at Soulard in three different stages:

6 A.M.–10 A.M. – The market is calm, vendors are excited, not many people shopping, i.e., very relaxing.

10 A.M.–2 P.M. – The market is nuts, vendors are bustling, there are so many people it is hard to move, i.e., very exciting.

2 P.M.–5 P.M. – The market is dwindling, the vendors are tired, there are fewer people, i.e., this is the best time to strike deals with vendors.

TOWER GROVE FARMERS' MARKET
tgmarket.org
Tower Grove Park, near the Pool Pavilion
South City
Saturdays, Mid-May–late October, 8 a.m.–Noon

This South City market has grown from a tiny experiment to become just about the biggest and most visited farmers market in the city, and that's mostly because it is varied and dynamic. It could also be because the guidelines for it insist that all things sold are raised, grown, or made within Missouri and Illinois.

Bring your reusable cloth bags and start filling them up with produce from farms like City Seeds, Centennial Farm, Our Garden, and Living Springs Ranch; eggs and lamb from Prairie Grass Farm; beef and pork from Hinkebein Hills Farm; baked goods (sweet and savory) from Companion and Four Seasons; coffee from Kuva; salamis from Salame Beddu; and an abundance of jams, salsas, pickles, cheese, soap, and new weekly treasures.

Don't be surprised to find local musicians playing or free yoga in the field just to the west. Twice a year the market hosts festivals, one in the beginning of the season and one in the fall. These festivals bring four times as many vendors as are regularly in attendance.

WEBSTER GROVES FARMERS MARKET
webstergrovesfarmersmarket.com
Intersection of Big Bend Blvd. and South Old Orchard Ave.
Thursdays, May–October, 3 p.m.–6:30 p.m.

WILDWOOD FARMERS MARKET
www.facebook.com/WildwoodFarmersMarket
Wildwood Town Center, at Fountain Pl. and Plaza Dr.
Saturdays, May–October, 8 a.m.–1:30 p.m.

FARMERS MARKET NOTES

_____

_____

_____

_____

_____

_____

_____

_____

WINTER FARMERS MARKETS

Most of the small markets close down after October, but these farmers markets remain open, at least once a month, until May.

KIRKWOOD FARMERS' MARKET
downtownkirkwood.com/farmers'-market.aspx
150 E. Argonne Dr.
Kirkwood
Open year round.
See entry on p. 101.

MAPLEWOOD FARMERS MARKET WINTER PANTRY
schlafly.com/bottleworks/farmers-market
Schlafly Bottleworks
7260 Southwest Ave.
Maplewood
Open year round.
See entry on p. 102.

For the winter months booths and vendors move inside the Bottleworks building.

SOULARD FARMERS MARKET
www.soulardmarket.com
730 Carroll St.
Downtown
314/622-4180
Open year round.
See entry on p. 103.

ST. LOUIS COMMUNITY FARMERS MARKET
St. John's Episcopal Church
3664 Arsenal St.
South City
Open the second Saturday of each month, November through April, 9 a.m.–1 p.m.

Many of the same vendors that sell at the Tower Grove Farmers' Market can be found here during the off season.

WINTER FARMERS MARKET NOTES

_____

_____

_____

_____

_____

_____

_____

_____

HOW TO TELL THE FARMERS FROM THE BROKERS

First and foremost, the farmers are generally pretty proud of their farms and, if it is not too busy, they are usually happy to talk to you about them.

Second, local farmers usually have a large quantity of just a few items—and these items are obviously in season.

Third, produce from small farms varies in size and color, and it's not covered in shiny wax.

Last, the small farms try to target a different kind of buyer than the brokers by growing heirloom or other hard-to-find varieties.

One more thing, sometimes farmers and brokers are one in the same. A farmer may have a bad crop or only a few items, so s/he will bulk up their selection with purchased produce.

RECIPES

SPRING

FRENCH BREAKFAST RADISH SANDWICH WITH RADISH SHOOTS AND ARUGULA VINAIGRETTE | SERVES 4

Breakfast of an open-faced sandwich of butter, radishes, and fresh herbs is a French countryside tradition. This recipe is a light lunch version of that classic.

Sandwich
8 pieces marble rye, toasted
4 T goat cheese
1 bunch French breakfast radish, thinly sliced
¼ c radish shoots (see note)
4 T arugula vinaigrette

Note: You want to get the freshest sprouts possible. The best sources are farmers markets or grocers specializing in local produce. Claverach Farms (available at Maplewood Market and Local Harvest Grocery) and Hot Skillet Farms (available at Tower Grove Market and Local Harvest Grocery) are two top local producers of radish sprouts.

Arugula Vinaigrette
1 c fresh arugula
2 T white onion, chopped
1 clove garlic, chopped
1 lemon, the juice only
¹⁄₃ c olive oil or grapeseed oil
salt and pepper to taste

Note: This vinaigrette recipe is extremely versatile. Replace the lemon juice with any kind of vinegar, or replace the arugula with any type of herb or mixture of herbs. Add a touch of honey or sugar if you want a little sweetness in your dressing. It keeps in the refrigerator for weeks.

Prepare the vinaigrette.
- Place arugula, onion, garlic, and lemon in blender.
- Blend until everything is a bit broken down.
- Open the top cap that rests in the lid of the blender and, while the blender is on, slowly pour in the oil.
- Add salt and pepper to taste.

Make the sandwich.
- Toast the bread.
- Spread 4 of the slices with 1 T goat cheese each.
- Lay radish slices on top of the goat cheese.
- Toss radish shoots in vinaigrette.
- Sprinkle mixture over the radishes.
- Top each sandwich with the unused slices of bread and cut into 4 triangles.
- Serve with soup, salad, or chips.

SUMMER

MISSOURI SUMMER SUCCOTASH (VEGETARIAN) | SERVES 6

This is my modern take on a Midwest classic. I created it while working as the chef at Mangia Italiano. The taste and texture really embody summer, and the parmesan gives it an Italian twist! It is equally terrific fresh off the stove at the dinner table, or chilled the next day at a family picnic.

6 ears of sweet corn
½ lb okra
4 lbs of ripe tomatoes, about 3 medium
3 T grated hard cheese, preferably Parmigiano-Reggiano
3 T olive oil
salt and pepper to taste

- Cut the corn from the cobs, cut okra into ½-inch rounds, and dice the tomatoes.
- Place each in a separate bowl.
- Place olive oil in large sauté pan on medium heat.
- Once oil has heated up, add the corn and sauté quickly, for about one minute.
- Add the okra, and sauté until it turns bright green, about another minute.
- Add the diced tomatoes, and cook until the tomatoes start to fall apart.
- Remove from heat. Add cheese, and salt and pepper to taste.
- Serve hot or cold as a side dish.

FALL

MUSTARD GREENS AND BLACK-EYED PEAS | SERVES 4–6

2 bunches mustard greens, washed and chopped
2 small cans black-eyed peas, rinsed
2 cloves garlic, minced
2 T olive oil
1 T apple cider vinegar
salt and pepper to taste

- Place oil into a large skillet, add garlic, and sauté slightly.
- Add greens, and cook until slightly wilted.
- Add black-eyed peas, and cook until warm.
- Add vinegar, salt, and pepper.

WINTER

ROASTED BUTTERNUT SQUASH AND CAULIFLOWER SOUP | SERVES 6

3 butternut squash
1 head cauliflower, cut into small florets
1 medium onion, chopped
3 carrots, peeled and chopped
2 T butter
4 cloves garlic, smashed or chopped
1½ teaspoons fresh ginger, peeled and minced
4 c vegetable broth
1 t salt (or to taste)
dash cayenne pepper (optional)
grated hard cheese (optional)

- Preheat oven to 400°.
- Cut the butternut squash in half lengthwise, and scrape out the seeds.
- Spray or rub a rectangular baking dish lightly with oil, and place the squash in it cut-side down.
- Put the squash into the oven, and set the timer for 30 minutes.
- Meanwhile, put the cauliflower florets into a small, oiled baking dish of their own.
- After the squash has cooked for 30 minutes, put the cauliflower in the oven, too.

- Bake, stirring every 10 minutes, until the cauliflower is beginning to brown and the squash can be pierced easily with a fork. They will probably be finished at different times.
- Remove each from the oven when done, and set the cauliflower aside.
- Allow the squash to cool until it's easy to handle. Scrape the flesh out of the skin and into a bowl. Discard skin.
- Use a fork or masher to mash the squash a little.
- In a large saucepan, sauté the onion with the butter until translucent.
- Add the garlic, carrots, and ginger.
- Cook until carrots begin to soften.
- Add the squash and the vegetable broth to the pan.
- Using a hand blender, blend the soup to a smooth purée. (If you don't have a hand blender, purée the soup in your blender in batches.)
- Reduce the heat to low, and cook for about 15 minutes.
- Add the cauliflower to the soup.
- Taste for seasoning. Add salt, cayenne, and cheese as needed.
- Cover and allow the soup to simmer until the cauliflower is tender.

SOFT-BOILED FARM FRESH EGGS

6 eggs

- Place eggs in small sauce pan, and cover with water.
- Bring to a boil, then lower to a simmer.
- Simmer for 3–5 minutes.
- Run under cold water until cooled.
- Peel and serve.

HERBS AND SPICES

Technically these aromatic wonderlands could fit with the specialty stores, but I think they deserve a chapter of their own simply because the quality of herbs and spices—even down to the salt and pepper—is so integral to anything cooks prepare. Herbs and spices take up such little space in a dish, yet they account for a large percentage of the flavor.

Most herbs and spices owe their flavors and aromas to the oils contained within. The oils can be adulterated, dry up, or lose pungency rather quickly. Even in dried herbs and spices, keeping the oils intact is the goal of a reputable manufacturer.

Quality fresh herbs can be found at farmers markets and other stores with large produce sections, and bear the same properties of other decent produce. Look for dark or bright green leaves with healthy, strong stems. I treat them almost as freshly cut flowers, storing them upright in water in the refrigerator. Fresh spices are brilliant in flavor and aroma, and you want them as freshly ground as is available to retain their lovely oils. When possible, I grind them myself.

Most dried herbs are irradiated (a process of exposing the herbs to radiation to kill bacteria and extend shelf life), so I try to stay away from these. As mentioned, even herbs purchased dried should taste as flavorful as possible. Don't we all have a memory of trying dried herbs from dusty bottles in the pantries of our youth, coming across years-old tarragon with little or no flavor, and perhaps years later still not knowing what the heck tarragon is supposed to taste like?

The flavor of dried herbs is more concentrated than that of fresh ones. When substituting dried versions for fresh, use only about a third of the amount the recipe calls for.

RECOMMENDED SPICE LIST

ALMOND EXTRACT – this tasty extract is great for adding a sophisticated flavor to baked goods.

ANCHO PEPPER, GROUND – sweeter and milder than regular chili powder, with a dark raisin-like flavor.

BASIL – buy fresh (or grow it yourself!); works well for pesto, pasta, anything with tomatoes, and even berries.

BERBERE – an Ethiopian spice blend consisting of chilies, ginger, basil, garlic, fenugreek, and a few other Ethiopian spices that serves as the base flavoring for many Ethiopian dishes.

CAYENNE – the ground powder of dried chilies; generally very hot, so use with caution—a little goes a long way.

CHILI POWDER

CORIANDER – the dried seeds of the cilantro plant, used often in Indian cooking, found in breads and sausages of Eastern Europe, and added to some beers for flavoring.

CURRY POWDER – there isn't just one curry powder—you will find such differing styles as:

- garam masala – sometimes just labelled *masala*, northern Indian style curry based on a cardamom, coriander, and black pepper blend, and probably the most popular in the U.S.
- hot curry – a turmeric-based curry with lots of peppers for heat.
- maharajah curry – known as the "premiere curry," it's also based on

turmeric, but features lots of cardamom and saffron, meaning it's generally sweet and very mild.

- massaman – a Thai mix featuring star anise and tamarind.
- sweet curry – generally mild, it hails from southern India and is based in turmeric, coriander, and cumin.

GUMBO FILÉ – the dried and ground leaves of the sassafras tree, used pretty much exclusively to thicken gumbo and give it that real "back woods" flavor. I like to sprinkle it on potatoes, add it to rice, or throw it into cooking lentils.

LEMONGRASS – best bought fresh, it will last for weeks in your refrigerator and even longer in your freezer. Great for tea, soups, and cooking beans or rice. (Note: Lemongrass itself is inedible. Keep it in large chunks while cooking and discard it before serving.)

MUSTARD POWDER OR SEEDS – my secret ingredient! A little mustard powder in your next vinaigrette adds amazing flavor and tang. Sprinkle on your breakfast potatoes for a different flavor and a wonderful texture.

OLD BAY – a spice blend, concocted near the Chesapeake Bay in the 1930s, which began as a crab seasoning and is now widely used for many types of seafood and even chicken.

PEPPERCORNS – the world's most traded spice adds a little kick to all sorts of food daily.

- black – the unripened fruit of the pepper plant, boiled then dried.
- white – the seeds contained within the ripened fruit of the pepper plant.
- green – usually found pickled or dried, the unripened fruits of the pepper plant.
- pink – the dried fruits of the Peruvian pepper tree.

RED PEPPER FLAKES

RUBS – stock up on rubs to have a multitude of flavor profiles at the ready.

SAFFRON – used for its spectacular color and its subtle earthy aroma, the small and expensive threads are actually the dried stigmas of a wild crocus native to and first cultivated in Greece.

SEA SALT – salt seems to be the hottest new cooking trend, with hundreds of new types, flavors, and colors suddenly available. Here are a few of my favorites:

- del gris – mineral rich "grey salt" harvested from the bottom of ponds; great for meat, root vegetables, and baking.
- flaked sea salt – briny and robust with a crunchy texture.
- fleur de sel – the top layer of sea salt derived from hand harvesting methods, prized for its delicate flavor.
- kosher salt – my simple daily salt; it dissolves weak and is fairly inexpensive.
- smoked salt – exactly what is sounds like, wonderful for meat and starches like potatoes.

TURMERIC – found fresh or dried and ground, used for its brilliant color (it will stain!) and earthy flavor.

VANILLA BEANS – sold whole or as a paste or powder.

CINNAMON – cassia, Ceylon, Indonesian, and Vietnamese.

ZA'ATAR – a popular Middle Eastern seasoning blend of sumac, thyme, and sesame used on meat or vegetables, or eaten with oil and bread.

SPICES SHOPPING LIST/NOTES

_____

_____

_____

_____

_____

_____

_____

_____

STORES

AFGHAN MARKET
3740 S. Grand Blvd
South City
314/664-5555
See entry on p. 176.

AKBAR
10606 Page Ave.
Olivette
314/428-1900
See entry on p. 197.

PENZEYS SPICES
penzeys.com
7338 Manchester Rd.
Maplewood
314/781-7177

Serious spice heaven! One divine outlet of thirty-nine Penzeys nationwide, they have just about everything you're looking for, and probably six different varieties of it. And while your sniffer's up there in the clouds, it's nearly impossible to leave the store without getting some serious down-to-earth spice education. You stand to learn more about sea salt and Vietnamese cinnamon than you ever thought there was to know.

It starts with the samples throughout in the store (for tasting and smelling!). Come here for a field trip of smells, and leave knowing the difference between Hot Paprika, Smoked Paprika, and Hungarian Paprika. Spices at this stratosphere are not cheap, but I can promise that the product will be fresh, and that will take your cooking oh so far.

Most of the products come in a range sizes, from I-just-need-it-for-tonight small to I-cook-a-whole-heck-of-a-lot big. These options make it really easy to shop here and keep your spices from getting too old. Caraway, Hint of Mint Hot Chocolate Mix, mahlab (the ground pit of sour cherry, it's a sweet and sour addition to breads, cookies, and biscuits), orange peel, pink peppercorns, shallot salt, and turmeric are just a few regulars that make it from Penzeys' shelves to mine.

The store also carries everything found in its popular mail-order catalog, a big plus, and is a good place to find an unusual and useful gift for just about anyone on your list (boxed assortments available for big spenders).

SEEMA ENTERPRISES & SEEMA WORLD TRAVEL
10635 Page Ave.
Olivette
314/423-9990
See entry on p. 201.

SOULARD SPICE SHOP
730 Carroll St.
Soulard Farmers Market, Downtown
314/783-2100

This quaint little shop inside the Soulard Farmers Market (see p. 103) is one of my favorites of all time. Housed in the middle, permanent portion of the market (the Grand Hall), they carry a wonderful selection of herbs and spices and sell them quite affordably in various sizes.

You can get oregano, thyme, chili powder, gumbo filé, and dozens of others in tiny (about two ounces, great for new recipes or for those of you who don't cook all that much), normal (about eight ounces), or giant (one to two cups, just right for ingredients you use often and for those of us who cook in bulk). They also sell various rubs and spice blends, many without salt.

Along with the spices, the ladies of Soulard Spice Shop sell olives, Volpi salami (see p. 60), and cheeses like havarti, cheddar, pepperjack, swiss, and mozzarella. They will slice it to order, or just cut off a nice hunk. Then there are the many, many ready-to-make mixes—for soups, stews, dips, pies, cookies, cheese balls, and drinks. They have salad dressings, preserves, salsas, vinegars, and sauces. A whole wall is dedicated to bulk coffee, and another one to loose teas. Like the spices, these items are priced right for stocking up.

Be careful and go early: on Saturdays it can be quite impossible to even get in the door.

URZI'S ITALIAN MARKET
5430 Southwest Ave.
The Hill
314/645-3914
See entry on p. 185.

VIVIANO AND SONS GROCERS
shopviviano.com
5139 Shaw
The Hill
314/771-5524
See entry on p. 186.

SPICE STORE NOTES

RECIPES

BBQ SAUCE

3¼ c ketchup
²/₃ c water
²/₃ c apple cider vinegar
½ c molasses
¾ c brown sugar
¼ c oil or butter
4 T paprika
1 T chili powder
1 T cayenne
1 T garlic powder
salt to taste

- Place all ingredients in a medium sauce pan. Heat until well incorporated.
- Use immediately, or store in fridge and use within two weeks.

MADRAS POTATOES

2 medium potatoes, boiled and sliced
2 T oil
1 t mustard seeds
½ t turmeric
1 t ground coriander
½ t cayenne
½ t salt
1 c water
2 t lime juice

- Heat oil in a sauté pan, add mustard seeds, and cook for a few seconds.
- Add potato and remaining spices. Cook for 3 minutes.
- Add water while stirring.
- Reduce heat, cover, and cook for 5 minutes.
- Remove from heat. Stir in lime juice.
- Let cool slightly before serving.

GUMBO! | SERVES 6

Make it vegetarian by leaving out the sausage and shrimp. Make it vegan by leaving out the sausage and shrimp, and replacing butter with oil.

¼ c butter
¼ c peanut oil
1 c flour
1 large yellow onion, diced
1 medium red bell pepper, diced
1 medium green bell pepper, diced
6 stalks celery, diced
2 T parsley, chopped
1 jalapeño or serrano, minced
4 cloves garlic, minced
1 T gumbo filé
1 T Cajun seasoning (equal parts salt, pepper, onion powder, basil, thyme, chili powder, garlic powder, and a touch of cayenne)
1 t cayenne
1 t paprika
½ lb Andouille sausage, sliced
4 qts seafood or chicken stock
2 c cooked (or canned) black-eyed peas (optional)
1½ c fresh okra, sliced
1 c corn, cut fresh off the cob
1 c tomato, chopped (out of season I use whole peeled tomatoes)
1 lb raw shrimp (preferably with heads on)
salt and pepper to taste

- In a large, heavy bottomed pot, heat butter and peanut oil.
- Add flour. Cook until roux (this mixture of fat and flour) turns a nice dark brown (somewhere between caramel and milk chocolate), stirring constantly, about 30 minutes.
- Add onions to the roux and cook until slightly soft.
- Add peppers, celery, parsley, and jalapeño. Cook until soft.
- Add garlic, spices, and sausage, making sure they all get nicely toasted.
- Slowly add slightly warmed stock to the pot, whisking feverishly (the slow add plus the whisking ensures a velvety gumbo).
- Add vegetables, beans, and shrimp.
- Stir until well-mixed. Simmer for about 30 minutes.

- Gumbo should be thick and full of flavor. Add salt and pepper to taste.
- Serve with freshly cooked greens (perhaps Garlicky Greens, p. 97) and brown rice.

GINGER VEGETABLE SOUP

1 t coriander seeds
1 t yellow mustard seeds
3 T oil
1 t curry powder (preferably Madras)
2 T fresh ginger, peeled and minced
1 medium onion, chopped
3 cloves garlic, minced
1 lb carrots, peeled and thinly sliced into rounds (about 4 cups)
3 small red potatoes, chopped
zest of one lime
5 c vegetable broth or water (or more)
juice of one fresh lime
plain yogurt (for garnish)

- Grind coriander and mustard seeds in spice mill to a fine powder.
- Heat oil in heavy large pot over medium-high heat.
- Add ground seeds and curry powder.
- Stir one minute, add ginger. Stir one minute more.
- Add onion and garlic, stirring frequently.
- Sauté until onions begin to soften, about 3 minutes.
- Add carrots and potatoes. Cook for a few minutes.
- Add 5 cups broth, and bring to a boil.
- Reduce heat to medium-low.
- Simmer uncovered until carrots and potatoes are tender, about 30 minutes.
- Cool slightly.
- Working in batches, purée in blender until smooth.
- Return soup to pot.
- Add more broth by the ¼ cupful if too thick.
- Stir in lime juice. Season with salt and pepper.
- Ladle soup into bowls, garnish with yogurt, and serve.

MEAT, POULTRY, AND GAME

We in St. Louis are lucky to have an awesome selection of fresh meats, poultry, game, and even preserved meats available to us.

Let me also call your attention to the lovely spread of local meats you'll find at farmers markets, which more often than not will be frozen. In this case, the meat is butchered, packaged, and then sold within a month. Just because it's frozen doesn't mean it isn't delicious.

Most small farmers freeze their meat because they don't have the luxury of getting their product to the market immediately or being able to ensure it will be properly refrigerated for the entire shelf life. Freezing guarantees customers a safe product, and it prevents costly spoilage. Farmers work on very thin margins and they have to protect themselves.

I'll be the first to tell you that I was initially skeptical of frozen meat, but straight-from-the-farm frozen has proven to be more flavorful than "fresh" stuff direct from the grocery store.

BEEF – available types include conventional, grass-fed, and organic.

BISON – known to be leaner than beef, and considerably more nutrient rich.

CHICKEN – I try to buy my chicken fresh, but some farms sell it frozen because it's more efficient to slaughter a lot of birds at once and then sell them slowly over a few months' time.

DUCK – most of what you find in St. Louis is frozen, but there are a few farmers in Soulard (see p. 103) and markets on Olive (see p. 211) where you can get duck fresh.

ELK – usually found frozen.

GOOSE – mostly found frozen.

LAMB – Missouri lamb is delicious and abundant. You can find almost any cut you desire, as well as lamb bacon and lamb sausage.

PORK – there are a few happy pig farms in Missouri—theirs is the best pork you will ever taste.

VENISON – brought in by local hunters and processed at small butchers, venison here is usually found frozen or as jerky.

NOTES ON MEAT, POULTRY, AND GAME

_____

_____

_____

_____

_____

_____

_____

_____

IS GRASS-FED BEEF REALLY BETTER?

We have all heard the horror stories about cows being raised in factory feed lots, but how does this affect the meat you buy at the grocery store and ultimately consume?

The life of seventy-five percent of beef cows in this country goes something like this: get born on a small ranch out west, nurse with its mother for six months, and graze on a pasture. Then the cow is weaned from both its mother and the pasture, and sent to a huge cow fattening facility or "feed lot." Here the cow spends the next year in extremely tight quarters with other cows, raw sewage, and bacteria. The feed lot life tends to lead to stressed out, weak, and unhealthy cows.

As if the conditions aren't bad enough, the cow is fed a harsh diet of corn feed that causes it to gain mass quickly, but wreaks havoc on its digestive system and health, necessitating the use of antibiotics. These antibiotics remain in the meat that eventually finds its way to our plates, which can be harmful. The overconsumption of antibiotics creates imbalances in one's digestive system, as well as leads to more, and more drug-resistant, bacteria. Fifty years ago, most cows heading to slaughter were four or five years old. Now, with these facilities and drugs, cows can be ready for slaughter in fourteen to eighteen months.

Grass-fed, i.e., pasture raised, cows live a very different life. These cows roam freely, eating a diet their bodies were built to digest, only given antibiotics if it is critical, and allowed to grow at their natural pace.

Grass-fed cows, and the workers who raise them, are generally healthier and happier than those stuck in huge cow factories. And guess what? The meat from these animals happens to be healthier, found to have up to sixty-five percent less fat and cholesterol, and more vitamin E, vitamin C, and Omega-3s.[1] Not to mention the flavor—sabroso!

On top of all the health benefits, eating locally grown, grass-fed beef is a boost to the local economy. When the farmers are doing well, everyone is doing well.

Last, but not least, grass-fed cows are usually sent to smaller slaughter facilities that treat the cows more humanely and pay more attention to the details that may escape notice in a more frenzied environment. It is against federal regulation, for example, to slaughter a cow that is unhealthy, but the inspections are few and far between in the larger facilities where they are slaughtering thousands of cattle a day.[2]

Though grass-fed beef may be a little more expensive, it is a worthwhile investment in things that matter.

[1] Jo Robinson, *Why Grassfed Is Best!: The Surprising Benefts of Grassfed Meats, Eggs, and Dairy Products* (Vashon Island, WA: Vashon Island Press, 2000).
[2] Robinson, *Why Grassfed Is Best!*

STORES

BAUMANN'S FINE MEATS
8829 Manchester Rd.
Brentwood
314/968-3080

Every time I shop at Baumann's, friendly employees pull me further into secret nuances of butchering and smoking processes. After sixty-seven years in business, these folks are masters in the ways of the meats, and still looking for new initiates. There are many that will have come before you. They are now loyal customers, many greeted by name.

Just like the old school butcher shop that it is, Baumann's makes their own jerky and sausage. These smoky and spicy treats are but one reason people keep coming back for more. Laid out in long glass cases, a full line of beef, chicken, and pork cuts—all fresh—harkens. Push past the steaks, pork chops, and chicken breasts to try their specialty, housemade sausage. Dive into Andouille, brats, salsiccia, chorizo, pork sausage, and tasso (a smoky Southern ham), all fresh and ready for your grill or cast iron skillet.

Baumann's is one of the few butcher shops around that carry local grass-fed beef (ground, t-bone, ribeye), available in the freezer case. The freezers are also stocked with their housemade sausages, as well as frog legs, twice baked

CELEBRATE OUR CITY.

When you go to the butcher, don't forget the pork steak. This cut of meat is fundamental to St. Louis style barbeque, and just plain special to this part of the country. If you want to give your out-of-town friends something uniquely local, grill up this steak and braise it in BBQ sauce.

potatoes, duck breasts, and stuffed peppers. They have a small inventory of frozen seafood, like shrimp, tuna, mussels, crawfish, and tilapia.

I love their "Everyday is a Holiday" smoked tenderloin or standing rib roast, which you can order (for delivery even) anytime. During the festive seasons they also sell smoked turkeys and green hams, along with traditional holiday offerings like brisket and fresh turkeys.

If you don't want to fuss with the mess, they will also make dinner for you. Check out their premade meatloaf, meat balls, and stuffed pork chops.

Like any good butcher shop, they carry great BBQ sauce (of their very own label), rubs, charcoal, and wood chips from Chigger Creek. (Chigger Creek is a small, family-owned company from Columbia, Missouri, that has been making more than ten flavors of wood chips and logs for over twenty years.) Let Baumann's make all your grilling dreams come true.

CARNICERÍA LATINO AMERICANA
2800 Cherokee St.
South St. Louis
314/773-1707
See entry on p. 155.

DIGREGORIO'S ITALIAN FOODS
5200 Daggett Ave.
The Hill
314/776-1062
See entry on p. 184.

FARMERS MARKETS
See entry on p. 100.

G&W
4828 Parker Ave.
South City
314/352-5066

Since 1965, the family at G&W has been churning out Bavarian style sausages using generations-old family recipes, with the motto: "Opened by the son of a Sausage Meister!"

This little store on Parker Avenue, tucked between car dealerships on Kingshighway Boulevard, sells about twenty-five varieties of German (and not so German) sausages including brats, knackwurst, salsiccia, chorizo, and Andouille. In the cold case, fine deli meats and cheeses await custom slicing. A dry erase board on the wall behind the counter notes what types of meats they may have hiding in back.

In addition to fresh sausage, the Meister has been making landjager (translated as "country hunter"), a semi-dry sausage akin to a meat stick, summer sausage (they have specially imported mustards to complement this), and bloodwurst, a peppered German salami. Don't miss the German imports such as candy, wonderful cookies, easy-to-make spatzle mix, spicy mustards, and briny pickles.

G&W is one of the last vestiges of the Old Country in our once very German city, but they have also done a wonderful job keeping up with the sausage needs of modern St. Louis and its contemporary ethnic enclaves over the years.

In the fall, they offer butchering services for area deer hunters.

HANLEN'S MEAT SHOPPE
11037 Manchester Rd.
Town and Country
314/966-8606

A friend who used to go here as a child first brought me to Hanlen's: "It was always so much fun to come here as a kid. You could take in a few pennies and come out with a huge bag of candy!"

Well, the candy is gone now but it's still fun to visit. Like a kid, I wanted to press my nose against the glass of the meat case to admire all the fresh cuts. They stock a full line of beef, pork, and chicken, but also elk (steaks, ground, and sausages), ground bison, and local venison (frozen in all cuts).

In the refrigerated case next to the raw meat, there's bacon (they smoke it themselves!), deli meats, and cheese, which they will slice to order, along with a few prepared food items. After you have picked up the family dinner or party food, grab a 5-lb bag of ground chicken (bones and all) for your pets. Dogs and cats will go crazy for this healthy alternative to kibble.

In the freezer, you can find the more curious meats (I mean…for the more curious cook) like elk, bison, and pheasant. The salty chorizo goes great with mussels, the kabobs are just waiting for the hot grill, the shrimp and crawfish round out the recipe for gumbo (see p. 120). Find the elements of a mini grocery on the shoppe's shelves: They stock charcoal, wood chips, barbeque and other sauces, salsa, olives, soup mixes, and even a small selection of beer and wine.

It can't go without being said that the staff retains the old-school butcher shop vibe and imbues every exchange with helpfulness and pleasantries.

IRISKIC BROTHERS MESNICA BUTCHER
5411 Gravois Rd.
Bevo
314/752-3488
See entry on p. 168.

JALISCO MARKET
Lotsie Depot Shopping Center
10086 Page Ave.
Overland
314/890-9898
See entry on p. 156.

LEGRAND'S MARKET & CATERING
legrandsmarket-catering.com
4414 Donovan Ave.
St. Louis Hills
314/353-6128

LeGrand's has been around for a long time, but not always under that name. It was Binder's Tom-Boy for decades, until about 1990 when it was bought by two LeGrand Brothers. Now the large store is half grocery, half butcher and deli counter, complete with some tables and chairs. At this counter you can order one of the fifty or so meat-piled sandwiches to eat immediately, or any cut of beef, chicken, or pork you so desire to take home and cook.

"There are just a few cuts ready for pick up," one of the owners, Joe, told me, "we prefer to cut everything to order—fresh and to the thickness each customer wants." These boys will do absolutely any cut possible if you give them a little lead time. They even get half of a grass-fed cow about once a month and offer a call-list for folks who want cuts of it. Call and ask for one of the two Joe's or two Jim's (I bet that's not confusing for them....), and any of the four will put you on the list for a personal phone call when they're about to order a cow.

This crew is also busy smoking and drying their own jerky; making BBQ meats (ribs, pulled pork, and pulled chicken); grinding beef; and making their own brats, sausages, and a host of sides for eating in or carrying out. Thinking meat? Make your own BBQ Sauce (see p. 119), and let LeGrand's do the rest.

They have a few little freezers near the counter full of specialty meats (lamb, veal, Cornish hens, and, in the summer, bison) and fish/seafood (tilapia, scallops, salmon, shrimp). The grocery part of the store has that small-family-grocery feel, and is usually actually staffed by sons, daughters, and wives of the owners. A smile and friendly hello when you walk in the door is virtually guaranteed.

LeGrand's is a wise old gem, the perfect place to stock up for a family cook-out, picnic, or tailgate. Or, just swing by to be transported back a good sixty years.

MEAT FAIR
2315 Chambers Rd.
North County
314/868-9118

Meat Fair doesn't have any signage outside—unless you count a giant handwritten one reading, "FREE SODA"!—so keep your eyes peeled. When my nephew and I walked in on a recent outing, he said, "What's that smell?" That, my young apprentice, is the smell of an old grocery store!

We were there to assess what makes this store a "Soul Food Grocery." St. Louis's Southern style is in full-swing here, and I was immediately drawn to the smoked ham hocks, smoked ham shanks, smoked turkey, and smoked just-about-everything-else.

As it straddles the Mason-Dixon Line, St. Louis is a rather Southern place, and this store has some real Southern selections that I've haven't seen in too many stores around here: hens, rabbits, chitterlings, delta syrup (a dark, sugar cane syrup with a rich flavor), hog heads, hog maws. Now most of these things need to be asked for by name, but there is all manner of soul food and its common ingredients out on the shelves—catfish (fresh and frozen), tons of biscuits (pre-made and mixes), dried black-eyed peas, big tubs of spices, frozen greens and corn, special seasonings and breading mixes, sweet potatoes, onions, and other nice produce. Even green peanuts!

PAUL'S MARKET
1020 N. Elizabeth Ave.
Ferguson
314/524-3652

The sign out front of Paul's proclaims, "The Biggest Little Steak Store in St. Louis." I'm not sure if that title is official, but I would say they're definitely in the running. This small neighborhood market has been butchering and selling meat since 1960. Paul's retains its small neighborhood feel, both in size and in attitude.

This vintage butcher shop prides itself on customer service and can get you anything you want as long as it comes from a pig, cow, or chicken. Looking for a bacon chop (a pork chop with the belly still attached), hanger steak (a wonderful and cheaper replacement for tenderloin), or a royal short rib? Call Paul's and place your order! To go along with the meaty offerings, there's huge selection of BBQ sauce, woodchips, and free advice on cooking all manner of meat.

Their deli case is stocked with chicken breasts, housemade Italian sausage and brats, and special and ordinary cuts of pork and beef, as well as deli meats and cheese hunks waiting to be sliced per your instructions. Prepared items, such as pasta salad, fried chicken, cooked meats, mac-n-cheese, and coleslaw, are made daily. (Beyond the deli case, you can buy all your conventional groceries and produce—coffee, toilet paper, onions, domestic beer, etc.)

Paul's Market is a great little piece of St. Louis history with a whole lot of character. A mini-museum on the walls tells their story through photographs and framed newspaper clippings.

PIEKUTOWSKI'S EUROPEAN STYLE
4100 N. Florissant Ave.
North City
314/534-6256

North City is speckled with small hints of the once thriving community, mostly evident in the ornate and beautiful architecture of the buildings that now lie neglected. This all but forgotten about part of our city still holds a few culinary gems. Piekutowski's is one.

On a little traveled part of North Florissant Avenue, you'll see the ancient sign hanging on the corner, boasting European style sausage. That's exactly what you'll find inside, along with a variety of pickles, mustards, pasta, spices, cheese, and deli meats. Stepping in the door of the store is like going back in time. Hmm—what is it about our butchers and days of yore?

Piekutowski's makes all their sausage in-house using the owner's family recipes dating back to when the shop opened in the 1940s. Specialties include their Polish style and Krakow sausages (apparently a hit with Pope John Paul II when he visited St. Louis in 1999). They also make beer salami, Italian sausage, bratwurst, and bologna. All of their cured products are sold wholesale, and you can find them at grocers around the city.

This is truly a must-see, must-do in St. Louis. Support these sausage makers and their old-school ways. Enjoy your encased meat just like Grandpa did!

THE SMOKEHOUSE MARKET
smokehousemarket.com
16806 Chesterfield Airport Rd.
Chesterfield
636/532-3314
See entry on p. 57.

SOUTH CITY MEAT (MESNICA)
5201 Gravois Ave.
Bevo
314/457-8107
See entry on p. 169.

EL TORITO
2753 Cherokee St.
South City
314/771-8648
See entry on p. 159.

VOLPI ITALIAN SALAMI & MEAT COMPANY
volpifoods.com
5263 Northrup Ave.
The Hill
314/772-8550
See entry on p. 60.

NOTES ON MEAT STORES

_____

_____

_____

_____

_____

_____

_____

_____

RECIPES

SPICE RUB | GOOD FOR ABOUT 6 RACKS OF RIBS, OR 2 PORK BUTTS, OR 4 CHICKENS

Good meat is great, and one way to make it even better is to cover it in a delicious spice rub. You can buy these pre-made rubs at many spice shops (see *Herbs and Spices* chapter on p. 112), or you can make one yourself. Try this:

½ c salt
¼ c chili powder
¼ c ground black pepper
¼ c cumin
¼ c brown sugar

- Combine all ingredients.
- Use immediately on any type of meat.
- Or, store in an airtight container for up to six months.

ROASTED CHICKEN WITH ROASTED GARLIC JUS | SERVES 4–6

1 whole chicken, cut into eight pieces
4 cloves garlic
2 T fresh rosemary
4 T olive oil
1 T salt
½ T pepper
6 cloves roasted garlic
½ c white wine
1 t butter

- Pre-heat oven to 400°.
- Purée garlic, rosemary, salt, and pepper in food processor. Smear on chicken pieces.
- Place chicken on a cookie sheet or in an oven-proof pan. Roast in oven for about 30 minutes, or until done.
- Remove chicken from oven, and place on a serving platter, saving the juices in the pan.
- Place pan with juices on the stove top, and add roasted garlic and white wine.
- Cook until reduced by half.
- Add butter, and pour over chicken.

BUTTERMILK FRIED CHICKEN | SERVES 4

1 whole chicken, rinsed well and cut into 10 pieces
2½ cups buttermilk, divided
6 eggs
6 T salt, divided
2 T freshly ground black pepper
3 c unbleached flour
1 c yellow mustard powder, such as Coleman's
2 t ground cayenne
lard or peanut oil

- Place the chicken in 2 cups buttermilk, and soak 1 to 12 hours.
- In a large bowl, whisk remaining buttermilk with eggs, 2 T salt, and pepper.
- In a separate bowl, mix together flour, mustard powder, cayenne, and remaining salt.
- Set a thick-bottomed pot, such as a cast-iron Dutch oven, over medium heat, and fill with 2 inches of lard or oil.
- Using the clean hand method[1], dip the chicken pieces first in the wet ingredients, then in the dry ingredients, and then once more in the wet ingredients.
- Dip all pieces before proceeding.
- Once the oil reaches about 350° (or when a test piece of chicken bubbles quickly), carefully place just enough pieces of chicken in the pan to cover the bottom.
- Be sure not to crowd the chicken.
- Flip the pieces as necessary, and fry until golden brown.
- Place a cookie sheet lined with paper towels in a 200° oven.
- Remove pieces as they are done frying, keeping them warm in the oven.

---

[1] By using only one hand in the bowl of flour and only the other hand in the bowl of milk and egg, this reduces the gunk build up on your digits.

QUICK CHICKEN STOCK | MAKES 2 QUARTS

2 chicken thighs
2 qts water
4 cloves of garlic

Use this chicken stock in the ramen recipe on p. 217.

- Place all ingredients in a pot, and bring to a boil.
- Reduce the stock to a simmer, and simmer for 45 minutes.
- Cool stock, then strain.
- Lasts for a week in the fridge and up to 6 months in the freezer.

FISH AND SEAFOOD

In the past ten years, the selection of fresh seafood in St. Louis has improved immensely, owing greatly to the eating habits of an influx of immigrants and the changing palates of the residents.

There are a few simple rules to keep in mind about fresh fish:

- Make sure it doesn't smell fishy. Fresh fish should smell like the water it lived in, like an ocean or lake.
- Make sure the eyes are clear. Cloudy, sunken eyes are the first sign that the fish has been dead for far too long.
- Make sure the skin and flesh are firm and not slimy or squishy.

Most seafood (mussels, oysters, clams, crabs, lobster) should be bought alive or frozen. These products have an extremely short shelf life, and this is the only way to guarantee their freshness (especially since we are smack in the middle of the country, quite far from any body of saltwater).

Mussels, oysters, and clams should go home with you alive and remain that way until you put them in the pot and cook them. Crabs and lobster can be butchered at the store if you want to save yourself the act.

"How do I know they are alive?" you may ask. Well, lobsters and crabs are easy. They will be moving—the more they are moving the healthier they are. Shellfish like mussels and clams are closed tightly when they are alive and well. Note that they will open up slightly when resting behind the seafood counter or in your fridge, but a little tap should send them back to tightly closed. If not, they are dead.

STORES

BOB'S SEAFOOD
8660 Olive Blvd.
Olivette
314/993-4844

Bob's used to reside in a tiny storefront in the University City Loop, but recently moved to a larger building on Olive Boulevard. There's no denying that Bob's smells like fish, but what else would you expect from a place that ships in fish every day? Along with their open-to-the-public store, they also supply many of the restaurants in this town.

Bob's is clean and simple. You walk in, and there are a few cases full of fresh fish. The selection changes daily, mostly based on the demands of the restaurants and the availability of the fish, but some things you are almost sure to find—halibut, salmon, tuna, swordfish, grouper, mussels, and oysters. A sizeable tank holds live lobsters.

Your seafood comes with over forty years of advice (everything from cooking tips to wine pairing) that all began with founder Bob Mephram's weekly road trips to the Gulf of Mexico, where he cultivated relationships with and an understanding of the work of fishermen. The growth of the business from small market stand to full-fledged store and butcher has gained respect for the quality of Bob's product and his team's fantastic hand butchering.

The store also sells frozen items, such as shrimp, crab legs, and crawfish, as well as a few dry goods, like spices, rice mixes, and sauces. You will most certainly find soft scallops for grilling and catfish for frying. You can always expect to discover something off-the-beaten-path here too, maybe uni (sea urchin), turtle, skate, or monkfish. Whether you are looking for a delicate poached white fish, hosting your own crab boil, or serving up a pot of hearty seafood gumbo, Bob's is your one-stop shop for all things fish.

OLIVE FARMERS MARKET
8041 Olive Blvd.
Olivette
314/997-5168
See entry on p. 215.

SEAFOOD CITY GROCERY
7733 Olive Blvd.
Olivette
314/721-6688

Seafood City sometimes feels a bit more like a zoo than a grocery store (field trip for the kids!). The last time I was there, I met a pile of live crawfish crawling around a large open air display in the middle of the seafood section, next to the live frogs and sea turtles. This place is very aptly named, as its fish population matches that of a small city.

Beyond the wriggling and swimming food, pick up all sorts of live mollusks here—clams, mussels, oysters, and snails all sit neatly stacked in fresh flowing water. Most of the seafood they carry is fresh (blue crab, oysters, clams, perch, mackerel, snapper, goat fish, jackfish, grouper, smelt, pike, lobster, eel, and carp—to name a few), but they also have a well-stocked freezer.

As a grocery store, Seafood City gives even the nicest Dierbergs a run for its money. The aisles are huge, clean, and well-lit. The shelves are well-stocked and well-marked (in Chinese, Korean, and English), making it super easy to get around and get what you want.

There is a meat department, with the usual Asian beef, pork, and chicken offerings, as well as fresh duck (just about the only place in town) and Korean-cut short ribs (sliced super thin for quick and easy cooking—best glazed in brown sugar and soy sauce).

Never had Filipino food? This is the place to go for the infamous banana catsup (bright red and tastes like ketchup but it's made from bananas), pickled green mangoes, or annato powder. Filipino cuisine, heavily influenced by Spanish culture, will blow your mind. Try some Filipino flan, the *longaniza* (a cousin of the famed Spanish chorizo), and the *escabeche* (fried fish that is then pickled), a tasty twist on the Mediterranean version.

Yes, come here for the awesome fish and seafood choices, but Seafood City is also a one-stop shop for Asian ingredients and a fine choice if you're just looking for a food adventure. You will come home with a few stories and most likely more than one impulse buy.

WHOLE FOODS MARKET
wholefoodsmarket.com
1601 S. Brentwood Blvd.
Brentwood
314/968-7744

1160 Town and Country Crossing Dr.
Town and Country
636/527-1160

Whole Foods Market is a nice place to buy expensive and fresh produce, fancy cheese, and otherwise quality ingredients. The hefty prices keep me away when it comes to general grocery shopping, though I do shop here regularly for seafood because of their guidelines for the fish they sell. Dubbed their "Quality Standards of Aquaculture," Whole Foods only buys farmed fish with standards that respect the ecology, the fish, and the surrounding wildlife. Their fished seafood must be caught by means of sustainable and responsible practices. Buying seafood and fish at Whole Foods saves me the time of searching for what is sustainable and safe before I go shopping, but this luxury isn't without costs.

NOTES ON FISH AND SEAFOOD STORES

_____

_____

_____

_____

_____

_____

_____

_____

RECIPES

CRAWFISH STUFFING (MIDWESTERN OYSTER STUFFING) | SERVES 10–12

This is my Midwestern take on traditional oyster stuffing. You can buy crawfish tail meat (raw or pre-cooked) or live crawfish at Bob's Seafood on Olive.

10 c crusty French bread, cubed
7 T unsalted butter
2 T bacon fat or olive oil
4 shallots, thinly sliced
6 stalks of celery, thinly sliced
1 lb crawfish tail meat (raw or precooked)
2 c chicken or vegetable stock
⅓ c dry vermouth
2 T fresh sage, chopped
2 T fresh thyme, chopped
1 t Tabasco or other hot sauce
salt and pepper to taste

- Preheat oven to 200°.
- Arrange bread cubes on a baking tray.
- Place in oven for about 20 minutes.
- Put 5 T butter and 2 T olive oil in a large skillet on medium heat.
- Add shallots and celery.
- Cook, stirring occasionally, until vegetables are soft.
- Add crawfish tail meat to pan.
- If precooked, simply warm the meat; if raw, cook until bright red.
- Add sage, thyme, salt, and pepper.
- Cook for a minute to release the flavors of the herbs, then add stock, hot sauce, and vermouth.
- Combine this mixture in a bowl with the bread cubes.
- Let stand for 15 minutes.
- Raise the oven temp to 400°.
- Grease an ovenproof pan with 1 T butter.
- Transfer stuffing into pan. Cover with foil.
- Bake for 30 minutes.
- Remove the foil. Drizzle with remaining 1T butter.
- Bake for 30 more minutes.

CRAB CAKES | MAKES 15 CAKES

1 lb crab meat
1 T oil
2 shallots, minced
2 red bell peppers, minced
2 yellow bell peppers, minced
6 ribs of celery, minced
⅓ c mayo
2 T Dijon
1 T horseradish
2 T Sriracha or other hot sauce
juice of 2 lemons
2 eggs
½ bunch parsley, chopped
3 c panko (see p. 210), and more for breading
salt and pepper to taste

- Drain crabmeat.
- Warm oil in a medium skillet, and add peppers, shallots, and celery.
- Sauté until soft. Set aside to cool.
- In a bowl combine crabmeat, mayo, Dijon, horseradish, hot sauce, lemon juice, eggs, and parsley.
- Mix lightly as to not break up the crab too much.
- Add the panko, salt, and pepper. Mix well and taste.
- Form crab cakes, and roll each in panko.
- Place a thin layer of oil or clarified butter on the bottom of a large skillet.
- Heat and then add crab cakes, flipping once the first side browns nicely.
- Once both sides are brown, drain on a plate covered with a paper towel.
- Serve with mixed greens and a creamy sauce.

BEER, WINE, AND LIQUOR

There is absolutely no shortage of wine, beer, and liquor stores in the St. Louis area, most of which could be considered *alcohol warehouses*. These giant places with open floor plans and high ceilings make it rather easy to get lost in a sort of "booze daze," without having consumed a drop. You wander around with wide-eyes, mouth-gaping, and feet-dragging, trying to understand how you could ever possibly taste every brandy, stout, absinthe, and sparkling something in the place. Each of these drink emporiums specializes in one or two things, be that beer or wine or bitters, and yet—that doesn't seem to diminish the overwhelming selection of everything else.

Once you have shaken off the haze, it's time to get down to serious beverage buying. You are in good hands. Every store highlighted here has helpful, knowledgeable, and enthusiastic employees prepared with tips, suggestions, and information on new or rare products.

STORES

FRIAR TUCK'S

friartucksonline.com
9053 Watson Rd.
Crestwood
314/918-9230

4635 Highway K
O'Fallon
636/300-4300

792 Gravois Bluffs Blvd.
Fenton
636/326-2359

In my mind, Friar Tuck's specializes in beer—though they won't commit to that. They claim to have "1000s of wines and the largest selection of spirits, anywhere." Well, I don't know about "anywhere," but they are oozing with booze.

The beer selection ranges from cans of local microbrews to 750ml Belgian white ales. They're all over the map in more ways than one. You'll drop in for a six-pack, and come out with a cart full of things you "just have to try." That happens to other people and not just me, right?

Friar Tuck's permits everyone's favorite "pick a six" option, where you get an empty six-pack container and fill it with whatever beers you want, thus creating the best sampler pack known to humanity. The beers are from all over the world, and prices vary by bottle. Take a brewery tour of Europe from your living room, or taste the best beers of St. Louis without having to remortgage your house.

Their wines are nothing to scoff at either, nicely displayed in three huge rows in classy wooden boxes. Don't let me forget the liquor. The selection is from A to Z and back again, and, of course, all the mixers you need too.

Pick up home-brew equipment if you get the itch to make your own beer, or thirst-quenching gift boxes for great presents. And for the worst impulse buyer in you, they have airplane-size bottles that will surely catch your eye: Think absinthe, baby Maker's Mark, Fireball. Best of all, they are open until ten most nights.

RANDALL'S

shoprandalls.com
1910 S. Jefferson Ave.
South City
314/865-0199

11000 Old Halls Ferry Rd.
North County
314/741-5100

14201 Manchester Rd.
Manchester
636/527-1002

10800 Lincoln Tr.
Fairview Heights, IL
618/394-9800

The curious decorations of all Randall's locations continue to amuse me even many years after they expanded their empire to South City. Walk into the warehouse-sized liquor store to find old cars, and creepy life-size animatronics towering over the hundreds of vodkas (not to mention other liquors), hundreds of beers, and over a thousand wines.

Each location of this boozy megastore is tailored to the neighborhood it resides in, keeping owner George Randall busy tweaking the selection at all of his four stores. That is no small task—these places are huge! Along with the almost excessive amounts beer, wine, and liquor, they stock all kinds of mixers, from small batch sodas to dozens of different bitters, and accessories like corkscrews, glassware, and fancy toothpicks.

Hard day at the office? Stop by Randall's! The insane selection and the weird decorations are sure to put a smile on your face before you even take a nip.

THE SCHLAFLY TAP ROOM

schalfly.com
2100 Locust St.
Downtown
314/241-BEER, x1

SCHLAFLY BOTTLEWORKS

schlafly.com/bottleworks
7260 Southwest Ave.
Maplewood
314/241-BEER, x2

The Schlafly empire, begun 22 years ago with a dream to make good beer, has grown into the largest locally owned independent brewery in St. Louis. Their valiant sense of adventure when it comes to beer making (try Pumpkin Ale, Tasmanian IPA, and Raspberry Coffee Stout), along with their stellar treatment of their staff and love of any and everything St. Louis, has earned them deserved popularity and loyalty. At this point you can buy Schlafly Pale Ale, Hefeweizen, Kolsch, and Oatmeal Stout just about anywhere beer is sold. But that doesn't make the Tap Room or Bottleworks unnecessary! These establishments are like living beer museums.

The Tap Room is located downtown in a beautiful turn-of-the-century brick building restored to its original glory and now housing three bars, a music venue, a dining area, and a glass-enclosed brewing operation so you can actually watch the beer at work. So go have a pint (please don't miss whatever is on cask), eat some of chef Andy White's inspired food, hear some local music, and take home a six pack—or even a keg.

Schlafly Bottleworks is the younger of the two locations, located inside of an old grocery store. Bottleworks is home to a farmers market on Wednesday afternoons (see p. 102), has a large bar with 16 taps, a giant patio, private rooms for events, a dining room, a glass-encased bottling floor, and a tiny beer museum documenting St. Louis's love affair with the bubbly drink.

The gift shop at Bottleworks also offers beer and kegs, but it doesn't stop there. They also sell T-shirts, glassware, hats, bottle openers, cozies, and even soap. These are some of the few places in St. Louis where you can saddle up to the bar, have a few pints, and then take beer home—enjoy it!

THE WINE AND CHEESE PLACE
wineandcheeseplace.com
7435 Forsyth Blvd.
Clayton
314/727-8788

9755 Manchester Rd.
Rock Hill
314/962-8150

14748 Clayton Rd.
Ballwin
636/227-9001

457 N. New Ballas Rd.
Creve Coeur
314/989-0020

The Wine and Cheese Place is much more than it sounds. Although they do have impressive offerings of both wine and cheese, plenty more fills the shelves, including tons of beer and spirits. The Rock Hill location alone boasts an inventory of 350 beers, while the Clayton location has more high-end wines. They all share the mouth-watering selection of food products: crackers and salami, dry pastas, olive oils, vinegars, pasta sauces, frozen pizza, coffees and teas, honeys, jams, candies, and spices.

The cheese in these stores is not to be missed—as if you could possibly walk past a giant open refrigerated case with one of the most daunting cheese displays in the city. The cheeses are not always well-marked, but the staff is extremely knowledgeable and very willing to talk you through your cheese purchase. Go ahead, try a little of everything before you buy. You can find domestic, imported, hard, soft, sweet, spicy, and herbed cheeses, then move on to a wide variety of salami, olives, pâté, bacon, smoked salmon, pancetta, and prosciutto.

Wine beginners will find staff members at the ready to guide them through the wine options. Wine aficionados won't be disappointed in the choices available. Just remember, this place doesn't stop at wine and cheese—go there for your grappa, sake, or any flavor of vodka.

THE WINE MERCHANT
winemerchantltd.com
20 S. Hanley Rd.
Clayton
314/863-6282

When you walk into The Wine Merchant, you are immediately presented with the sale rack. This row of bottles is just the start of a wonderful journey into wine.

Right past the sale rack is the cooler, full of imported and American farmstead cheeses and preserved meats. The staff here is very proud of their variety of cheeses and will let you sample any of them, so don't hesitate to ask.

The main portion of the store is full of racks and racks of wine, Burgundy being their specialty. The reds and white are intermingled, but separated by country or region. The American wines are separated by grape varietal. Many of the wines are from boutique producers, meaning you will find some unique bottles in the mix. If you're lost, the staff is quite willing to help.

If you're still lost, The Wine Merchant offers wine classes four times a week with certified wine educators. Once a year, they offer a seven-week course based on the famous wine textbook, *Windows on the World*.

Beyond their exquisite wine selection, the Wine Merchant carries sparkling wines, liquor, spirits, and beer. The beer is cold (great for picking up just before the dinner party) and the whisky selection is extensive. Some of my favorite spirits they carry are Chouffe Coffee liqueur, Nocello, Cachaça, and different types of grappa.

To go with your drinks, they have glassware, crackers, olives, chocolate, eggs, bacon, salami, cigars, and even books.

NOTES ON BEER, WINE, AND LIQUOR STORES

RECIPES

MUSSELS IN WHITE WINE | SERVES 4

2 lb mussels
2 T oil and 2 T butter
2 large shallots, thin sliced
6 cloves garlic, thin sliced
2 c white wine
1 t tomato paste
1 T butter
1 oz chives, chopped
red pepper flakes, salt, and pepper to taste
1 lb pasta, cooked al dente

- Clean mussels: scrub shells, remove beards (the black, hair-like growths sticking out of the shell), and discard any that are not closed tight.
- Sauté shallots in oil until slightly soft.
- Add garlic, and stir a few times.
- Add wine, and heat to a boil.
- Add tomato paste, and stir.
- Add mussels—in one layer if possible. Cover.
- Cook until all mussels are open, about 3 to 8 minutes.
- Remove cover once most mussels are open. Be careful not to overcook mussels, or they'll become chewy. (Not all mussels will open; discard those that don't.)
- Continue to cook a few minutes longer to reduce the liquid a bit.
- Remove from heat.
- Add butter and scallions. Stir.
- Add pasta. Stir until mixed.
- Pour into a big bowl and place in middle of the table.
- Serve with plenty of grilled or toasted bread.

BRAISED BEEF OR PORK

This recipe can be also be used for tamale filling! See page 162.

3–4 lb piece of pork/beef shoulder, or butt (bone-in is fine)
spice rub recipe (see p. xxx)
2 T olive oil
1 medium onion, coarsely chopped
4 c beer, apple cider, or white wine

- Rub meat with spice the night before you want to braise it. Cover and place in the refrigerator.
- Preheat oven to 325°.
- Heat a large Dutch oven or a heavy oven-proof pot on burner, and add olive oil.
- Sear off all sides of the meat in the Dutch oven/pot until they are brown.
- Add chopped onion and liquid. Cover.
- Put in the oven for 3 to 4 hours (about an hour per pound), until the meat falls apart.
- Don't let liquid completely evaporate. Add more if needed.
- Once meat is falling apart, remove from oven and remove cover.
- Let meet cool until you can handle it.
- Pull meat apart using two forks until it is flaky.

MEXICO AND LATIN AMERICA

St. Louis has seen a slight increase in immigrants from Central and South America in the past few years, but their presence has been here for decades. A majority of the St. Louis Latino population is Mexican, but there are also notable numbers of Ecuadorians, Brazilians, Hondurans, and Salvadorans. It is impossible to generalize about the range of Latin American food styles, but you can be sure to find the spiciness of hot chilies and the brightness of citrus represented.

This chapter focuses primarily on Mexican cuisine because it is the most prevalent in our city. Situated between two continents and two oceans, Mexico is a large country with many different types of food. Its cuisine is a multi-layered pastiche of the ancient foods of the Mayan, Aztec, Toltec, and Zapotec peoples combined with the foods introduced by European conquerors. In the dishes of modern Mexico, you'll see native ingredients like chilies, squash, pumpkin, turkey, tomatoes, corn, chocolate, and vanilla along with the Spanish/European contributions of wheat, pigs, cows, goats, citrus fruit, rice, and onions.

Mexican cuisine can be split up into six regions:

- CENTRAL – has an emphasis on chicken, pork, vegetables, and dairy, and a generally mild flavor.

- WEST CENTRAL – has a bit more spice, along with tropical fruits, tequila, tacos, corn, and wheat.

- GULF – has a heavy Spanish influence, with an emphasis on plantains, coconut, pineapples, and nuts.

- NORTH – has a relatively mild flavor, but often with a smoky edge. The main starch is wheat, and the main protein is beef.

- YUCATAN – heavily influenced by the Mayans, with a large amount of native and ancient foods, plus a lot of chicken, turkey, and pork.

- OAXACA – the smallest geographical region on this list, but with the most diverse flavors. Oaxaca is famous for dried chilies, spices, *mole*, tamales, chocolate, and *coloradito* (a famous type of red mole).

INGREDIENTS AND PRODUCTS

The stores in this chapter are not 100% Mexican. Many other Central American items can be found on their shelves and in their dairy cases. As you'll see even more starkly in the other ethnic chapters, the grocers of St. Louis, and the products they stock, are rooted in the similarity of regional cuisines and the needs of immigrants to the United States, and not so much in the political, religious, or geographic divisions that exist eleswhere on the globe.

MEAT AND FISH

CARNITAS – pork cooked until it's falling apart. Buy it fully cooked and eat it with tortillas and salsas.

CHICARRÓNES – fried pork skins. Eat on tacos and sandwiches.

CHORIZO – pork sausage, very flavorful and a bit spicy, and deep red in color (it's made with chilies). Find it fresh (must be cooked before eaten) or cured (eat right out of the package).

PIG, ALL PARTS

SKIRT STEAK – cooks quickly for taco or quesadilla filling, it's sometimes available from the store already marinated in spices and chilies.

TONGUE – braised with onions and chilies for hours, until soft

TRIPE – used in the famous soup, *menudo*.

CHEESE

QUESO ASADERO/OAXACA – a white stringy cheese, close to mozzarella, great for melting.

QUESO BLANCO – a very soft, creamy cheese that comes in a tub.

QUESO CHIHUAHUA – much like queso oaxaca, well-suited for melting.

QUESO COTIJA – similar to feta, good for crumbling in a salad or over corn.

QUESO ENCHILADO – a semi-hard cheese that has been stored in chili purée, giving it a bright red and slightly smoky rind.

QUESO FRESCO/RANCHERO – a semi-soft, subtly flavored cheese; doesn't melt well.

PRODUCE

CALABAZAS – small, green summer squash.

CHAYOTES – light green squash puckered at one end, they can be roasted or even stuffed.

CHILIES – an abundance of varieties, dried and fresh (see p. xxx for more detail).

CILANTRO – a bright, kicky herb, related to parsley and carrots, used across Latin America.

GUAVAS – tropical fruit that are green on the outside, and generally a creamy pink or red inside when ripe.

HUITLACOCHE – a puffy grayish corn fungus that turns black when cooked! A delicious delicacy that grows on the outside of ears of corn.

JAMAICA (HIBISCUS FLOWER) – used mostly to flavor drinks, available dried whole or powdered.

JICAMAS – tan, tough-skinned tubers with a mild, sweet, crispy white flesh. Eat raw in salads or salsas, or boiled like a potato.

LIMES – the citrus zing beloved in Latin American dining.

MANGOES – available in many varieties, ripe when soft.

NOPALES – cactus pads, sold fresh or canned, eaten raw or sautéed, used for salads, salsa, or tacos. If bought fresh, be sure to cut edges off and scrape spines off with a knife.

PAPAYAS – large and delicious tropical fruit. They ripen easily in a brown bag until green exterior turns yellow or pink. Their flesh is soft when ripe and deep orange in color.

PLANTAINS – banana-like tree fruits, but much less sweet and a lot more starchy. Slice and smash the green ones for frying; add the ripe ones to favorite dishes. Ripe ones have the texture of ripe bananas, but with a mild and sweet flavor. Chop up and add to hash browns. Slice them longways and fill with cheese before baking. Or, mash them and add flour; cook them like potato cakes.

PRICKLY PEAR – the tart fruit of a cactus, purple in color and round in shape. Peel before using.

TOMATILLOS – tart fruits that look like small green tomatoes with papery husks, they can be blended into a salsa raw, or cooked into a sauce or soup.

YUCCA, CASSAVA – versatile and starchy tubers (see p. 160).

CHILIES

AJI' AMARILLOS – moderately hot and fruity yellow chilies, mostly found canned or dried in the States.

AJI' MIRASOLS – moderate to very hot yellowish red chilies, mostly found canned or dried in the States

AJI' PANCAS – dried chilies with a smoky, sweet, semi-hot, and lasting flavor, great for sauces.

CAYENNES – slightly smoky, spicy, and tart chilies, found fresh as small thin red peppers, but mostly used dried and powdered.

CHILES DE ÁRBOL – looking much like cayennes, these chilies are mostly found dried, and used to make salsa and the well-loved tortilla soup.

CHIPOTLES – smoke-dried jalapeños, often packed in the very flavorful adobo sauce.

GUAJILLOS – slightly sweet, dark, and robust chilies of just above medium heat, found dried, often used to make salsa or in cooking meat.

HABANEROS – one of the hottest chilies known, use with caution.

JALAPEÑOS – the familiar small green chilies used mostly raw in salsas, they range from moderately spicy to fairly spicy. Once smoke dried they're known as chipotles.

SPICES, SAUCES, AND CONDIMENTS

ACHIOTE – ground annatto seed. It has a subtle flavor, but gives food a beautiful red color.

ADOBO – a mix of herbs, spices, and citrus that gives body and complex flavor to any dish, found as a paste or powder.

CANELA – cinnamon, beloved spice used in sweet and savory Mexican dishes.

CHILE CON LIMÓN – a mix of salt, dried chilies, dried lemon and lime, and citric acid. It's used to sprinkle on fruit and corn, delivering a deliciously spicy and salty complement to the sweetness of fruit.

CUMIN – popular spice in Mexican food, pairs well with meat and is great in chili, found whole or ground.

HOT SAUCES – Some of my favorite brands are Tapatio, El Pato, Cholula, El Yucateco, and Valentina.

MAGGI SEASONING SAUCE – made from vegetable protein extracts, this ubiquitous sauce bring a new dimension to sauces, stews, and soups.

MOLE – the Mexican equivalent of curry: a complex sauce with an average of twenty ingredients (chilies, spices, and perhaps dried fruits, seeds, and chocolate), made differently in every household, and eaten with meat.

OREGANO, DRIED – Mexican oregano is a little different than its Mediterranean cousin, a bit more biting and peppery, a terrific addition to soups.

DRY AND PACKAGED GOODS

BEANS, REFRIED – pinto or black.

BEANS, WHOLE – white, red (kidney), black, pinto, garbanzo, *habas* (favas)

CHILIES, DRIED

HOMINY – hard corn (maize) treated with an alkaline solution to break down the outer hull, leaving it to look like puffed corn. It's found canned or dried, and is wonderful in soups and stews.

MASA – a ground cornmeal dough used to make tortillas, pupusas, gorditas, and tamales, can be found dried, instant, or fresh and ready to use.

PAN DULCE – sweet pastries that come in interesting shapes and colors.

TORTILLAS, FRESH – corn or flour, there is absolutely nothing like a fresh tortilla.

TOSTADAS – fried corn tortillas, a crispy base on which to pile ingredients.

MISCELLANY

CAJETA – caramel made with goat's milk, delicious on pastries and ice cream.

CHOCOLATE – found mostly in "table chocolate" form, meaning the chocolate has been combined with sugar and spices and formed into bricks, perfect for melting in milk and serving with breakfast.

CORN HUSKS – for tamales.

CREMA – a close relative of sour cream, but thinner and a little less sour.

DULCE DE LECHE – caramelized sweetened condensed milk, bought in a can or a bottle, a common Mexican flavoring.

JUICES, SODAS – uniquely Mexican beverages, many in tropical fruit flavors.

VANILLA – a native plant to Mexico and Central America, the vanilla extract used in most of the lovely desserts and cookies of this region.

NOTES ON INGREDIENTS AND PRODUCTS

_____

_____

_____

_____

_____

_____

STORES

CARNICERÍA LATINO AMERICANA
2800 Cherokee St.
South St. Louis
314/773-1707

5412 S. Grand Blvd.
South City
314/481-3665

10128 St. Charles Rock Rd.
St. Ann
314/427-3254

Recently voted "Best Mexican Market" by the _Riverfront Times_, the Cherokee location has become a cornerstone of the entire Cherokee Street community, Latino and non-Latino alike. Located on the corner of Cherokee and California, in the middle of what is referred to as "Little Mexico," you will recognize this store by the beautiful mural on the Cherokee side of the building that evokes a laid back afternoon in the homeland. Once you enter, you're hit with the smell of cooking meat, the sound of upbeat Ranchero music, and the sight of a few dozen piñatas smiling down at you (well, some look a little menacing).

The refrigerated section is stocked with tortillas, lots of cheeses, _crema_, yogurt, sodas, and juice, and most importantly, frozen _masa_, the dough used to make tamales. If you don't want to make it yourself, this is the only way to buy it premade (though making it yourself is quite easy, see the recipe on page 162). Their dry goods consist of most Mexican staples: dried and canned beans, juice mixes, chocolate, spices, and dried chilies.

Carnicería means butcher shop, and that's the most exciting part of this place. Pass the lunch counter, with its mountain of *chicharrónes* (basically, pork rinds), to get to the butcher counter. Here you will find traditional Mexican meat cuts like *arrachera* (thinly sliced and chili-marinated skirt steak), as well as pork sides and backs. You can also find shrimp and fish, but don't overlook the housemade chorizo.

The huge sign on the building exuberantly claims *Mexico Viva Aquí!* (Mexico Lives Here!). Twice a week, you can board a shuttle here that will take you to a bus in St. Charles that will take you south of the border—all the way to central Mexico!

The second and third locations of Carnicería Latino Americana opened not too long ago on South Grand Boulevard and St. Charles Rock Road. They have all the same groceries as the Cherokee location—and the same great butcher counter full of pork backs, cows' feet, flank steak, nopal (cactus) salad, and the wonderful housemade chorizo.

Don't forget to grab a Mexican Coke (made with real cane sugar instead of corn syrup like American Coke) for the road.

JALISCO MARKET
Lotsie Depot Shopping Center
10086 Page Ave.
Overland
314/890-9898

Cabeza de Puerco? Looking for a whole pig's head you can simmer for hours to make the amazing soup, *pozole* (don't forget to shave it and remove all whiskers). Or, if that's not your style, how about *lengua de res*—cow tongue braised with chilies and onions, chopped and ready for tacos?

This Mexican market, named after the central western state best known for its tequila production, has a lot more meat than just heads and tongues. Grab some *costillas de puerco* (pork ribs) for your next backyard BBQ, *arrachera* (thinly sliced skirt steak) for a quick weekday meal, or *chuleta de puerco* (pork chops) for your next date night. I love the housemade chorizo sautéed with onions. Serve it with refried beans, scrambled eggs, salsa, and tortillas for a breakfast your family won't soon forget. Standing wide-eyed and close to the case of this meat counter brings a giant smile to my face, exploring the possibilities in my mind as I fog up the glass.

Kick your condiment awareness up a notch here (and at all Latino markets, really). You'll discover bright red and flavorful hot sauces, whole pickled jalapeños (putting those nacho slices to shame), and the wonderfully rich lime-flavored Mexican *mayonesa*.

Their small but bright produce section includes the Mexican essentials of roma tomatoes, white onions, nopales, tomatillos, poblanos, and *calabacitas* (very firm and flavorful small zucchinis). Sauté these veggies and throw them in a warm tortilla, or chop them all up and add them to a stew with some purple hominy (or make pozole, see p. 161), which you can find next to the produce in one pound bags. I can already smell the deliciousness cooking!

Jalisco is one great market, brimming with real Mexican flavor, fresh meat and produce, and shelves of inspiration.

MALINTZI MEXICAN AND CENTRAL AMERICAN MARKET
3831 Woodson Rd.
Overland
314/428-2075

Malintzi, named from an inactive volcano in southern Mexico, has a little bit of everything. When you walk in a small food counter greets you offering delightfully traditional southern Mexican food: tacos, *tortas* (sandwiches served on soft white bread, meat of choice, pickled jalapeños, *mayonesa*, lettuce, cheese, and salsa), and *huaraches* (named after their shape—a sandal— thick hand-formed corn tortillas, toasted and topped with your choice of meat, grated cheese, salsa, avocado, lettuce, and onions). We all know it's a good idea to not shop on an empty stomach!

Pressing on after your snack, you'll find a butcher counter selling mostly beef products from nose to tail. Cheeks, ribs, *tripa* (tripe), liver, shank, *arrachera*, and ox-tail are all available fresh. Then mosey over to the small but very inexpensive produce section for potatoes, limes, onions, garlic, jalapeños, cabbage, and the holy grail—ripe avocados. Don't skip over the tomatillos, tiny bulb onions (with a sweeter and more subtle flavor than green onions), and *calabacitas*.

The dairy section has a few curiosities and a few must haves. (Note: Those are sometimes the same thing for me!) First marvel at the shelf stable milk (comes in a box like soy milk, and its' perfect for camping, baking, and just having in the pantry for milk emergencies) and the very firm *queso fresco* (it's the cheese that won't melt no matter what you do to it!). Then, grab *queso Oaxaca* (the original string cheese, wonderfully salty and chewy), *crema* (Mexican sour cream, but thinner and sweeter), and *queso Chihuahua* (creamy white cheese with a mild cheddar flavor, great for melting).

Finally, move on to the dry goods and fill your cart with plantain chips, *Sabritas* (chili and tomato flavored potato chips), the cheapest dried beans you'll ever find, prayer candles, spices, chocolate, and all kinds of sauces. Come once for the adventure, return for the grocery bargains.

LA MORENA
14234 Manchester Rd.
Manchester Center
Ballwin

This tiny place transports me back to my mid-twenties when I studied in Mexico—it's a ringer for the small grocer down the street from where I lived in Guanajuato. Americans might tend to call it a "hole in the wall," mostly because of its size, but towns in Mexico are littered with stores like this, as the megamart hasn't quite grabbed hold there.

Unlike the corner stores or 7-11s of the U.S., the corner stores of Mexico stock real and fresh food, everything you need to make a meal. I used to walk a few buildings down, buy zucchini, onions, cilantro, and eggs for breakfast, or tortillas, beans, and jalapeños to make my dinner. La Morena, too, is also the right place to swing by for the makings of a tasty dinner.

And if you don't feel like making a meal, consider any of these happy treats: *cacahuates japones* (crunchy coated "Japanese" peanuts flavored with soy sauce), a box of Jumex juice (I love mango), or a Bubu Lubu bar (a chocolate covered marshmallow and strawberry jelly candy bar). If it's cold outside, select a box of Abuelita or Ibarra table chocolate: Take it home, pull out a chocolate puck, slam it against the counter to break it up, melt it into a few cups of milk, and enjoy the best cup of hot chocolate you've ever experienced.

To round out the shopping experience, they sell what you need for cleaning the bathroom, washing your hair, or doing the dishes.

EL TORITO
2753 Cherokee St
Cherokee
314/771-8648

A great general store and restaurant rolled into one! The far west part of the store has a big kitchen, food counter, and numerous tables, where they serve *comidas* (complete meals) for lunch and dinner. The simple menu options are straightforward and include the expected meat in sauce, beans and rice, and tortillas. *Muy auténtico* (very authentic), they will tell you from behind the counter, and my tastebuds strongly agree.

The back part of the store is the butcher, stocked with beef, pork, chicken, and a bit of seafood. On the weekends, it's worth wading through the wall of customers to pick up the fresh corn tortillas kept warm in a giant warmer back there.

The middle of the store holds the groceries (cans of anything you need) and produce—basics like avocados, onions, nopales, carrots, cabbage, *calabaza*, mangoes, papaya, and cilantro, generally of good quality and at very affordable prices. I especially enjoy El Torito's bulk section where I go for huge bags of my favorite dried products: chilies, dried shrimp, and tamarind pods.

The far eastern portion of the store shelves the cooking equipment, clothes, bed sheets, CDs, jewelry, and knick knacks. The cooking equipment section is not to be missed. It's where to get huge pots (for tamales), citrus juicers, peelers, tortilla presses, and griddles.

Don't miss the food cart right when you walk in the door, selling chicharrónes and fruit (mango, watermelon, and others) on a stick sprinkled with chili and lime. A truly Mexican experience.

NOTES ON MEXICAN AND LATIN AMERICAN STORES

_____

_____

_____

_____

_____

_____

RECIPES

SALSA MEXICANA | YEILDS ABOUT 2 CUPS

6 ripe roma tomatoes, seeded and diced
½ yellow onion, diced
1 small jalapeño, minced
2 T cilantro, chopped
juice of two limes
salt to taste

- Combine all ingredients and eat immediately.
- Or, save in the fridge for up to a week.

MASHED YUCCA | SERVES 4

2 lbs fresh yucca
water for boiling
6 T olive oil
7 cloves garlic, minced
½ small yellow onion, minced
juice of two limes
salt to taste

- Peel and cut the yucca into big cubes, removing any woody pieces from the center).
- Add yucca to boiling water, and cook until you can pierce through with a fork.
- Drain, and mash with a fork.
- While the yucca is cooking, heat olive oil on medium heat.
- Add onions, and sauté until translucent.
- Add garlic, and sauté until soft.
- Remove from heat, and pour over the mashed yucca.
- Add lime juice.
- Eat immediately.

NEWEST TREASURE: YUCCA

Shopping with a friend not too long ago, he pointed at a long brown tuber and said, "What is that, and what do I do with it?" Um…"I will find out!" It turns out it was yucca, native to Brazil but eaten throughout Central and South America.

Once identified, I set out to learn how to cook it and found it's usually mashed and served with a garlic sauce, simple and delicious. Turns out yucca is yummy.

POZOLE ROJO | SERVES 4-6

2 c dry hominy
3 cloves garlic
½ yellow onion, chopped

2 shoulder steaks, about 1½ lbs
4 carrots, chopped
½ yellow onion
5–7 dry guajillo chilies, destemmed

package of tostadas or tortilla chips
one bunch (or bag) or radishes, quartered
¼ head of cabbage, chopped
3 T Mexican oregano

- Soak hominy overnight, then rinse.
- Place rinsed hominy in a medium pot with 3 cloves of garlic, ½ yellow onion (chopped), and water to cover. Bring to a simmer.
- Simmer hominy for about 2 hours, covered and undisturbed.
- Once cooked through, drain and set aside.
- While cooking hominy (or after hominy is cooked and set aside), place whole steaks, chopped carrots, and whole half onion in a large pot with 3 quarts of water.
- Bring to a simmer.
- Simmer ingredients until the steak is cooked tender, about an hour.
- Pull out the steaks and set aside to cool slightly. Once cool, chop into bite-size pieces.
- Add chilies to the pot and simmer with the vegetables until completely soft, about an hour.
- Once chilies are soft, pull out chilies and onion from the pot and place into the blender (or use an immersion blender).
- Blend to create the lovely smooth base of the soup. You will probably need a little water from the pot.
- Return base to the pot, add in hominy and cooked steak. Simmer for a few minutes until well incorporated.
- Serve immediately with tostadas (broken into smaller chips), chopped radish, Mexican oregano, and chopped cabbage on the side, for adding to the soup to taste.

TAMALES | MAKES 15

cornhusks

Masa Dough
2 c masa
½ c lard or butter
1 t salt
1 t chili powder
hot water if needed
Note: Make it vegan by using vegan butter, and coconut oil instead of lard.

Vegan/Vegetarian Filling
(for meat filling see p. 149 and use the pulled pork/beef recipe)
1 can hearts of palm, drained
1 t oil
½ large onion, finely chopped
½ c Mexican beer
½ t cumin
½ t chili powder
salt to taste

Salsa Roja
3 dried pasilla or guajillo peppers
1 t oil
1 clove garlic, chopped
1 c water
salt to taste

Make the dough first.
- Beat lard in standup mixer until light and fluffy.
- Add salt and chili powder, then add masa ½ c at a time, adding a bit of water if the dough is too thick.
- Set aside.

Next, make the filling.
- Place oil in sauté pan. Once hot, add onions and sauté until soft.
- Then add the hearts of palm and spices. Stir until hearts of palm are slightly caramelized.

- While still cooking, add beer and begin to shred the hearts of palm.
- Add salt to taste.
- Set aside.

Next, make the salsa for on top.
- Cut open the peppers, and discard stems and seeds.
- Turn high heat on a sauté pan or griddle, add oil, and lay peppers skin side down.
- Heat peppers until they give off a smoky flavor—browned but not burnt.
- Flip peppers over, and warm other side.
- Add chopped garlic to pan, and sauté for a few minutes.
- Put peppers, garlic, and water in a blender.
- Purée until smooth.
- Put through a fine mesh strainer. Add salt.
- Serve immediately, or save in the fridge for up to two weeks.

Finally, assemble the tamales.
- Soak corn husks in warm water for at least 30 minutes (you can also do it overnight).
- Rinse a corn husk and lay it on your work surface.
- Spread a thin layer of masa dough on the inside of the husk.
- Place about 2 T filling on dough.
- Fold dough up and around the filling.
- Once filling is completely encased, fold corn husk around the tamale to protect it.
- Repeat.
- Place tamales in a steamer, or in a large pot with about one inch of water and a plate on the bottom (to keep the tamales out of the water).
- Cover with lid, and steam for 15 to 30 minutes.
- Unwrap and enjoy with salsa.

MEXICAN WEDDING COOKIES | MAKES 2 DOZEN

2¼ c flour
¾ c finely ground almonds (or almond flour)
2/3 c powdered sugar, plus more for dusting
pinch of salt
1 c butter
2 T maple syrup
1 t vanilla extract

- Sift dry ingredients, and set aside.
- In a stand up mixer, cream shortening and maple syrup.
- Once it's light and fluffy, add vanilla.
- Add dry ingredients slowly, in four batches, fully incorporating before adding more.
- Once all together, divide the dough in 2, and refrigerate for 3 to 4 hours.
- Preheat oven to 350°.
- Line baking sheets with parchment paper.
- Roll 1 T dough into balls, and place on baking sheet.
- Cook until just beginning to brown, about 12–15 minutes.
- Remove from oven, and let cool slightly, about 15 minutes.
- Roll in powdered sugar.
- Cool the rest of the way on a wire rack.

BOSNIA, THE BALKANS, AND EASTERN EUROPE

When South City was at a low point in the 1990s, a wave of Bosnian immigration energized the area's sagging neighborhoods. This has created quite a diverse, but concentrated, world of Bosnian food and culture. From tiny corner butchers and amazing bakeries to full-blown groceries, the Bosnian settlement has provided St. Louis the unique opportunity to taste its many flavors.

The Bosnian population in St. Louis, centered in the Bevo area, is the largest outside of Bosnia and Herzegovina. These are largely Muslim refugees who fled their country under religious persecution during civil war and have found a haven in the ethnic-patchwork community of South St. Louis, helped by the efforts of the International Institute on South Grand. The institute offers services to all new immigrants, including job training, English classes, counseling, refugee resettlement, and tons of other helpful programs designed to ease the transition and educate existing communities.

Bosnian cuisine sits comfortably amidst Mediterranean, Middle Eastern, and Central European influences, creating a delightful mix of flavors. And bread is at the center of this cuisine. Whether it's served as a sandwich, on the side (fluffy and crusty, or flat and chewy), or as a flaky pastry containing delicious blends of meat and cheese, fresh homemade breads are the pride of all Bosnian stores. Beyond the bread, familiar ingredients like beef, chicken, lamb, tomatoes, potatoes, cabbage, beans, bell peppers, plums, and feta-like cheeses form the foundation of most Bosnian dishes. Dishes are always washed down with strong, sweet, and gritty Turkish coffee.

INGREDIENTS AND PRODUCTS

In Bosnian, Balkan, and other Eastern European Stores, highlights include preserved foods (fish, sausage, pickles), beautiful fresh breads (flatbreads, ryes, pumpernickels, and many more), and meat pies.

MEAT AND FISH

BACON – Bosnian bacon is deliciously smoky—and just salty enough.

BEEF – many Bosnian stores offer only a few different cuts of beef.

CEVAPI, CEVAPCICI – the national sausage—rather, dish—of Bosnia, traditionally made with beef, black pepper, cumin, garlic, and bread crumbs.

FISH, CANNED, TINNED, SMOKED – smoked fish from cans goes great on crackers.

GOVEDJA KOBASICA – a smoked beef salami.

LAMB – a staple in Bosnian dining.

MEAT PIES – tasty treats to eat on the go or bring home for lunch or dinner.

OFFAL AND ORGAN MEATS – liver, sweetbreads, tripe.

PASTRAMA – a jerky-like smoked beef sausage.

SUJUK – spicy, smoked beef sausage.

VEAL – bone-in or boneless steaks.

SPICES, SAUCES, AND CONDIMENTS

AJVAR – an eggplant-pepper-tomato condiment to treasure (see p. xxx).

JAMS AND SYRUPS – blueberry, fig, raspberry, sour cherry, strawberry, and more.

PICKLES – beets, cabbage, carrots, cucumbers, and more.

SPICES – paprika, thyme, Vegeta (commonly used vegetable-based spice mix).

MISCELLANY

KAJMAK – Bosnian version of sour cream.; a thick cheese similar to cream cheese.

OLIVE OIL – many varieties, in large sizes, at incredibly low prices.

PEPPERS – many styles in jars, especially roasted red peppers, some with paprika, and all surprisingly affordable.

TEAS – chamomile, elderflower, rose hip, and more.

NOTES ON INGREDIENTS AND PRODUCTS

_____

_____

_____

_____

_____

_____

BEFRIEND THIS CONDIMENT: AJVAR

As I wandered up and down the aisles during my first visit to a Bosnian store, not knowing what to look at first, a jar of bright red paste caught my eye. The color was so brilliant.

Even though I couldn't read the ingredient list, I knew what was inside from the pictures of eggplant, peppers, and tomatoes dancing across the label.

I took that first purchase home and soon had a lifelong friend. Ajvar is slightly sweet, very savory, and a bit spicy. Bosnians use it mostly as a spread on bread, but I have happily enjoyed it on pasta, in a ratatouille, as pizza sauce, and as a sausage accompaniment.

Ajvar comes in hot and mild.

STORES

EUROPA MARKET
5005 Gravois Rd.
Bevo
314/481-9880

The window displays of this store may be empty, but that's no reflection whatsoever on the clean, brightly lit, and well-stocked grocery inside. Europa Market has changed over the years. It started as a packed, somewhat messy, store, but is now sleek and totally modern, with an almost disconcerting amount of space. This wide open store greets you with a wall of cookies and packaged pastries along the south side, perfect compliments to the Bosnian drink of choice, Turkish coffee.

For the mostly Muslim Bosnian community, the non-alcoholic choices of coffee and tea serve as the social vehicles for time with friends and family—taken with strawberry-filled mini croissants, _lokum_ (basically an eastern European version of the chewy Turkish Delight), or the delightful fruit-topped and chocolate-covered cookie of the *Delicje* brand. These folks are serious about the sweets eaten with their caffeinated drinks. You will not ever be far from a cookie, chocolate, or candy in a Bosnian grocery. (If you need something savory, grab a popular spinach and cheese pie (*burek*) from the freezer section.)

Ever wanted to venture a taste of potted meat or canned pâté? This is your place. Slice and sear a luncheon loaf and serve it with breakfast instead of sausage, or pull the chicken pâté out of the can and display it on your next cheese plate next to the grainy mustard and cornichons. Don't be afraid to at least browse the large selection of sardines, mackerel, or tuna, perhaps adding one to your next pasta or pizza. I can't stop: Imagine a chili with Bosnian smoked beef; use Bosnian feta on your next salad; grate Livno (a dry yellow cheese reminiscent of Gruyère) on your pasta; or substitute *pavlaka* for sour cream.

IRISKIC BROTHERS MESNICA BUTCHER
5411 Gravois Rd.
Bevo
314/752-3488

When you walk in the door of this authentic (and aromatic) Bosnian butcher shop, a powerful blast of spices descends upon you like an aromatherapy spritz at the spa. It always puts me under the magic spell of hunger!

Mostly broken English is spoken here, but don't let that deter you—they are always eager to help you get what you need. Or maybe sell you something you don't!

The clean and modern butcher case is full of beef and lamb cuts and my personal favorite, lovely housemade *suduk* (or *sujuk*)—a spicy smoked beef sausage. The friendly man behind the counter gave me a taste the first time I went in. Heavy smoking of meats runs deep in the ways of the Bosnian butcher, so the smoked ribs, *govedja kobasica* (a smoked beef salami), and the jerky-like *pastrama* are virtually black with smoky flavor. At Iriskic Brothers the butchering room is behind glass and in full view from the counter, providing a deliciously voyeuristic opportunity to watch things happen.

There are also a few aisles of stocked groceries including lots of juices, sparkling water, jars of pickles (cabbage, beets, carrots), candy, European chocolate, cookies, pasta, tea, coffee, and an assortment of cheeses and creams.

SOUTH CITY MEAT (MESNICA)
5201 Gravois Rd.
Bevo
314/457-8107

Mesnica means butcher in Bosnian and, since the largest part of the St. Louis Bosninan community is Muslim, that means pretty much exclusively beef, lamb, veal, and sometimes chicken in the butcher shops. South City Meats and similar storefronts are full of completely recognizable cuts, like steaks and stew meat. It is fresh, and very affordable. How's boneless veal steak for $3.99/ pound, bone-in veal for $4.99/pound, and beef shank for $3.19/pound? Don't miss the offal either, like beef sweetbreads, liver, and tripe.

This is the only place in St. Louis I have found uncooked *cevapi* (also spelled *cevapcici*), considered the national dish of Bosnia and Herzegovina. It's a traditional sausage spiced with black pepper and cumin that's usually sold cooked and vacuum sealed (at least in the U.S.). Here at South City Meat the *cevapi* is freshly ground and stuffed, the real deal.

Last, but not least, my favorite item for sale here: giant pieces of smoked beef. The smoked beef of Bosnia is a source of pride and joy for the new immigrant (perhaps a clue to why they chose to settle in St. Louis), and they have brought their time-honored techniques with them. These cuts of beef are brined, rubbed, and then smoked for a long time, resulting in a very dry, very smoky, very dark end product. By custom, it's served on small finger sandwiches for breakfast, or as a midday snack with ajvar, cheese, and vegetables. Try it in place of sausage in your gumbo (see p. 120), or throw it in the next batch of risotto you cook up.

This butcher has more than just meat, there is a cooler full of dairy—yogurt, milk, cheese—and that other staple of the Bosnian household, fresh bread. Bosnians make over seventy types of bread, but here at South City Meat I only noticed three. No problem though, they have about twenty-five different jams for you to choose from including apricot, rose hip, plum, and fig. Your bread will never be boring with these spreads.

For those of you who go through olive oil like water, you can buy a big can of olive oil for under $10, and even a giant jar (and I mean giant) of roasted paprika peppers for about the same price. You will also find the obligatory juices and an overwhelming sparkling water selection, all much cheaper than Perrier.

ZLANTO ZITO
4573 Gravois Rd.
Bevo
314/752-3004

Meat pies! They sell fabulous bread, but the real reason to come here is meat pies! Walk in, go straight to the counter, and ask, "What kind of meat pies do you have today?" Once the woman behind the counter leaves to warm (yes, warm) your pie (or pies) of choice, then you can browse the preserved meats in the cooler, the twenty different kinds of Turkish coffee, the fruit filled croissants, and the chocolate.

And do get back to the bread. Bosnian bread comes in—pardon this—a *smorgasbord* of varieties: wheat, white, some light and fluffy, and some more like other European breads (ciabatta or French baguette). It's worth a spin around the wall of bread at Zlanto Zito.

By this time your meat pie will be ready. Take your pie in its Styrofoam home to a place you can safely eat it (or share it, if you are generous), and flip open the container to find this is not like most savory pies. This is a meat and cheese pie to die for—a buttery, flaky pastry dough (similar to phyllo) stuffed with delicious cheese, meat, and/or potatoes, rolled into a long tube, curled into a oval shape, and baked to perfection.

You will need napkins.

NOTES ON BOSNIAN, BALKAN, AND EASTERN EUROPEAN STORES

_____

_____

_____

_____

_____

_____

RECIPES

SMOKED MUSSEL DIP

1 tin of smoked mussels
8 oz cream cheese
juice of one lemon
1 T Worcestershire
1 t Tabasco or other hot sauce
2 t horseradish
salt and pepper to taste
½ bunch of parsley, chopped

- Place everything, except parsley, in the food processor.
- Pulse until slightly smooth.
- Taste, adjust seasonings, and then add parsley.
- Pulse one last time.
- Serve chilled or hot, with crackers or bread.

SOPSKA SALATA | SERVES 4
Named for the Bulgarian region of Shopi, from where the salad originates.

4 tomatoes, chopped
2 bell peppers, chopped
1 red onion, chopped
1 hot pepper, minced
2 T oil
salt to taste

½ c feta
1 T chopped parsley

- Mix tomatoes, bell peppers, onions, and hot pepper in a bowl with salt and oil.
- Top with feta cheese and parsley before serving.

BOSNIAN COFFEE (TURKISH COFFEE) I SERVES 2

6 oz water
2 t Turkish (finely ground) coffee
1 t sugar

- Put all ingredients in a small saucepan, or the more traditional *dzezva* (a small copper coffee pot with a long handle).
- Stir until well mixed, and bring to a boil.
- Remove from heat, and stir for about 30 seconds.
- Return to the heat, and boil a second time.
- Make sure a foam builds on the top.
- Serve in small demitasse cups or espresso cups.
- To be extra-traditional, serve with rustic, Bosnian-style sugar cubes. Dip the cubes in the coffee occasionally and suck on them.

LEBANON AND THE MIDDLE EAST

The term "Middle Eastern Cuisine" applies to the dishes of a large number of countries, including Iran, Iraq, Saudi Arabia, Afghanistan, Turkey, Syria, Lebanon, Israel, and Jordan. St. Louis may not have Lebanese-specific groceries, but the largest percentage of our population with Middle Eastern roots, hails originally from Lebanon. (The current mayor has Lebanese ancestry.) This part of the world is known as the "cradle of civilization," a place where people have been farming and cooking for millennia.

It is difficult to characterize the expansive territory and diverse cultures simply, but here are four things to keep in mind. First, many foods are common to most of these countries, and are or have become commonplace in American eating as well. Think: olive oil, sesame seeds, dried fruits, rice, couscous, chickpeas, yogurt, and pita breads. Secondly, Middle Eastern food tends to be heavily spiced, making Middle Eastern markets wonderful places to discover and buy spices. Third, in one word: Stews! Finally, remember that the majority of people in and from the countries of the Middle East follow halal and kosher diets because of religious rules and customs.

INGREDIENTS AND PRODUCTS

MEAT

HALAL MEATS – meats prepared in accordance with Muslim laws dictating how animals should be treated and slaughtered, similar in style and substance to Jewish kosher laws.

KOSHER MEATS

LAMB – a major part of the Middle Eastern diet, most halal butchers have it fresh and will cut it to order.

CHEESE AND DAIRY

FETA – crumbly goat's milk cheese with a pungent flavor.

KEFIR – a fermented milk drink, reminiscent of liquid yogurt and a great source of probiotics and other healthy bacteria.

LABNA – See recipe on p. 179.

YOGURT – consumed daily in Middle Eastern cultures, though not necessarily for breakfast. It's also used to prepare and garnish all types of sweet and savory dishes.

PRODUCE

FIGS – usually only found dry, they can be eaten raw or reconstituted in water or broth. Fresh ones are expensive, but worth the money.

GRAPE LEAVES – usually sold packed in brine, used to make *dolmas*, stuffed grape leaves (rice and flavorings, with or without meat, wrapped in the leaves).

SPICES, SAUCES, AND CONDIMENTS

HONEYS

ORANGE BLOSSOM WATER – an aromatic, even perfume-y, liquid, made by distilling bitter orange flowers, used to flavor breads, desserts, and even cocktails.

POMEGRANATE MOLASSES – a sweet, tart, and thick syrup made from pomegranate juice. Use in drinks, salad dressings, and glazes for meats, or pair with cheese.

PRESERVES – apricot, fig, orange, pear, plum, pomegranate, strawberry, walnut, and more.

ROSEWATER – a fragrant distillation of rose petals, used to flavor desserts, drinks, candies, and breads.

SYRUPS – in flavors "exotic" for Americans: orange blossom, rose, hibiscus, pomegranate, and more.

TAHINI – a sesame seed paste, used in making hummus and baba ghanoush.

ZA'ATAR – a popular seasoning blend of sumac, thyme, and sesame used on meat or vegetables, or eaten with oil and bread.

DRY AND PACKAGED GOODS

CHICKPEAS – garbonzo beans, dry or canned, perfect for making hummus or adding to soups and stews.

COUSCOUS – grains of semolina wheat flour, bought dry and boiled to make a delicious side dish. Couscous is rather plain tasting, so it is ripe for any flavorful additions

LENTILS – tiny legumes that come in many colors and types, usually found dried.

MISCELLANY

BABA GHANOUSH – a delicious dip made of roasted eggplant, garlic, tahini, olive oil, and lemon juice. Spread on sandwiches, or use as a dip for pita bread, crackers, and veggies.

FALAFEL – fried ground chickpea patties, traditionally served in pita with yogurt sauce. Buy a dry mix or ready-made patties.

HALVA – a dense, flaky dessert made of ground sesame seeds mixed with sugar and a flavoring.

HUMMUS – a flavorful dip made of chickpeas, olive oil, garlic, tahini, and lemon juice. Add to sandwiches, or use a dip for carrots, cucumbers, or bread.

NUTS – pistachios, cashews, almonds, and others, raw, roasted, and seasoned.

PHYLLO – thin, flaky dough, used by layering with melted butter and wrapping around a filling (e.g., spinach pies) or baking in a casserole. It's usually bought frozen in square sheets, but you can also find it in cup shapes and other fun shapes.

PITA – a round flat bread that comes in a few different sizes and textures, served whole, cut up for dipping, or split in half and stuffed for pocket sandwiches. Pita pairs well with falafel, hummus, and other bean dips.

SESAME CANDY – a simple and delicious candy of sesame seeds sweetened with sugar and honey.

TEAS – all kinds, but mostly black. These are very tea-heavy cultures.

TURKISH DELIGHT ("LOKUM") – a gummy candy available in interesting flavors like bergamot orange, lemon, rosewater, and more.

NOTES ON INGREDIENTS AND PRODUCTS

_____

_____

_____

_____

_____

_____

STORES

AFGHAN MARKET
3740 S. Grand Blvd.
South City
314/664-5555

A shining star of most Middle Eastern markets is the coffee and tea section—and Afghan Market is no different. Rows of vacuum packed grounds, mostly in the style of finely ground Turkish coffee, sidle up to brightly colored boxes of loose black teas. Coffee and tea replace alcohol as the social beverage in these Muslim communities, and they take their beverages seriously. Witness the ornate coffee urns, tea kettles, and other serving vessels. Cups and saucers are beautifully decorated.

You can't have coffee or tea without sweets, so be sure to peruse the cookie aisle that's amply stocked with treats unfamiliar to most of us: cookies filled with dates, cookies sandwiched with spiced cream, and Turkish Delight. Or, make your own sweets with a host of interesting ingredients: They sell four kinds of raisins (green, Thompson, golden, and sultana), dry mulberries, and flavor extracts you won't see anywhere else (chioo, khus, ice cream, mango, and nutmeg). The selection of flours would make any gluten-intolerant person blush (mung bean, millet, chickpea, and lentil, just for starters).

This is another place to stock up on spices affordably, most here happen to be imported from Indian and Pakistan. The frozen section even has Indian entrees and appetizers, like samosas and curries. Check out the cold case for a few kinds of yogurt drinks, labna marinated in olive oil, duck eggs, and two interesting cheeses in particular. One is labeled Arabian Cheese—it's firm and delicately flavored salty cheese, like a fresh farmer's cheese. The other is labeled Syrian Cheese—it's chewy and slightly stringy, with a mild flavor.

And, as you check out, grab a few dates from the bin on the counter to eat in the car!

BAGHDAD MARKET
3730 S. Grand Blvd.
South City

Right next door to Afghan Market on South Grand Boulevard, Baghdad Market is a similar Middle Eastern marketplace full of lovely teas, spices, legume flours, cookies, candies, and dried beans—so many dried beans! This shop boasts a halal butcher counter with beef, chicken (including whole), lamb, and goat (already in chunks) available.

You'll find most of the same products as next door, but a couple interesting things should be called out. First off, the roasted watermelon seeds. (I know, I know, we were all told to spit them out as children or else a watermelon would grow in our bellies.) Not just tasty, these little guys are full of B vitamins, magnesium, and essential amino acids. Second, try the dry fava beans. Make them into a hummus, a wonderful ham and bean soup, or a fava bean version of falafel—all delicious!

Baghdad Market has a great cookware section, right next to the tea and coffee kettles, filled with metal spoons, stainless steel pots, and skillets of all sizes. And, of course, don't overlook the treats. There are lots of dates and figs in all kinds of containers, big and small, a dozen different types of *halva* (ground sesame seeds mixed with sugar and a flavoring to make a dense and flaky candy), and absolutely delectable, delicately sweet sesame cookies.

THE VINE
3171 S. Grand Blvd.
South City
314/776-0991

St. Louis has been deeply impacted by the Lebanese immigration of a few generations ago, but unfortunately most of the Lebanese specific groceries have been assimilated into broad based grocery stores. The Vine is one-of-a-kind, the only standing Lebanese grocery in the city.

The south half of this store, on the International District of South Grand, is a restaurant that sells prepared and deli foods to order. The menu consists of mouth-watering falafel, chicken and beef shawarma (a sandwich made of slowly roasted, spiced meat), meat and spinach pies, hummus, tabouleh (a salad of bulgur wheat, parsley, onion, and tomato), and delicious housemade baklava.

The store half of The Vine stocks the usual rosewater, olive oil, and rice, as well as an amazing selection of lentils, nuts, grains, preserved fruits, sesame candies, flours, and spices. I love to come here for fresh pita. For the cocktail (or mocktail) enthusiast, there's orange blossom water, date syrup, and pomegranate molasses—perfect for fun concoctions.

Along with a small selection of produce, you can find all cuts of halal chicken, beef, lamb, and goat. They may have only a few things on display, including ground beef, whole chickens, goat tongue, and beef liver, but there are signs for the prices of every cut of meat you could imagine, e.g., even lamb head for $4/pound.

The Vine is a perfect place to try out salty Syrian cheese, very mild Arabian cheese, or trade your Philly cream cheese in for Puck brand cream cheese. You will also find jars holding marinating labna the size of golf balls.

Before you leave, grab yourself some halva and candy-coated chickpeas for dessert—they have a wonderful subtle sweetness that American candies have not even considered.

NOTES ON LEBANESE AND MIDDLE EASTERN STORES

_____

_____

_____

_____

RECIPES

BABA GHANOUSH | SERVES 8

3 medium eggplants
1 c parsley
juice from one lemon
¼ c tahini
3 cloves garlic, chopped
3 T olive oil
salt and pepper to taste

- Preheat oven to 400°.
- Prick eggplants with a fork all over and place on a baking sheet.
- Bake until flesh is really soft, about 30 minutes, flipping once.
- Peel, and discard stems and skin.
- Cut flesh into big chunks.
- Place the eggplant and all the rest of the ingredients into the food processor.
- Purée until smooth. Taste and season appropriately.
- Serve in a bowl topped with olive oil.
- You can also top with pine nuts or black olives for a little more flair.
- Smear on a sandwich or scoop up with warm pita bread.

LABNA

Labna is creamy and delicious, something like yogurt cheese. Use it like you would either cream cheese or sour cream—so versatile *and* good for your digestive tract.

1 large tub of yogurt (I use whole fat Greek yogurt, but really you can use anything)
1 t salt
olive oil
juice of one lemon (optional)
3 T fresh mint, chopped (optional)

- Line a colander with cheese cloth, leaving some hanging over the edge.
- Stir salt into yogurt, and place in lined colander.
- Gather the ends of the cheese cloth and tie to form a bag
- Hang the bag from the kitchen faucet, or anywhere on the counter with a bowl to catch the drippings, for somewhere between 12 hours and two days.

- Once done, remove labna from cheesecloth.
- Eat immediately, or cover with olive oil in a container with a lid and place in the refrigerator. Will keep refrigerated for up to 2 weeks.
- Optional deliciousness: Stir in lemon juice and mint when you first add the salt.

ROASTED CAULIFLOWER TAHINI | SERVES 4–6 AS A SIDE DISH

1 head cauliflower, broken into florets
2 T olive oil, divided
4–6 cloves garlic, chopped
¼ c tahini
2 T lemon juice
½ t salt
¼ c water

- Toss cauliflower with 1 T olive oil and salt, then spread in a single layer on a baking sheet.
- Bake at 350° for about 20 minutes, stirring twice.
- Meanwhile, in a small saucepan, sauté garlic in remaining oil until fragrant, being careful not to burn it.
- Take off heat, and stir in tahini, lemon juice, and water.
- Add more water if it isn't creamy enough for your tastes.
- After 20 minutes baking in the oven, the florets should still be firm, but tender enough so you can pierce them with a fork without any trouble.
- When done, place the florets in a large bowl, pour the tahini sauce on top, and toss to coat.
- Serve with crackers, as a side dish, or on top of a bed of lettuce.

ITALY

It's no secret that Italian food infiltrated St. Louis food culture decades and generations ago. The first Italians came to St. Louis for work once clay deposits were discovered in the area in the late 1800s. An ongoing Italian influence is seen in grocery stores and on restaurant menus, but it remains undiluted in "The Hill" neighborhood in South City. Here the streets are lined with Italian groceries, ice cream parlors, bakeries, eateries, and the like. Sometimes you even have the pleasure of hearing Italian spoken on doorsteps and sidewalks. Italian food has as many styles as it does provinces, but mostly Sicilians and northern Italians founded The Hill, so the styles of these disparate regions predominate.

Just for your sensory refreshment: Italian cuisine is known best for delicious cheeses, fresh and dry pastas, well-made oils (especially olive oil), cured meats, and the fervent use of tomato products.

INGREDIENTS AND PRODUCTS

MEAT

PANCETTA – Italian bacon, often rolled up, sliced thin. This meat has been cured, but not smoked, so it has a slightly different flavor than its American cousin

PROSCUITTO – cured and dried pig thigh, always sliced paper thin, prosciutto tastes best with melon or olives.

SALAMI AND OTHER PRESERVED MEATS – genoa, finnochiona, soppressata, bresaola, filzette, and many more.

SALSICCIA – a spicy sausage, you can find it fresh or frozen.

CHEESE

FRESH MOZZARELLA – a soft, subtly flavored cheese.

GRATING CHEESES – asiago, parmesan, grana padano, pecorino, and similar.

MASCARPONE – the Italian version of cream cheese, but the flavor is much smoother and a bit sweeter.

PARMIGIANO-REGGIANO – the name means "the king of cheeses," and is aptly named. If you buy one cheese at an Italian market, it should be this wonderful, hard, grating cheese. Parmesan is a cheese not made in Italy that imitates the recipe of Parmigiano-Reggiano.

PROVEL – a St. Louis concoction, a white melting cheese with a very distinct texture. (It's not the most appetizing texture, that of melted plastic, but St. Louisans love it!)

RICOTTA – the Italian version of cottage cheese, with much smaller curd and a bit sweeter, used for pasta fillings and sweets.

SPICES, SEASONINGS, AND CONDIMENTS

CAPERS – the pickled buds of the caper tree, used for their saltiness in salads and pastas.

PESTO – a paste usually made from basil, pine nuts, and olive oil that makes a perfect topping for bread or pasta.

TORANI SYRUPS – flavored syrups used for making Italian sodas.

VINEGARS, BALSAMIC – Italy is well-known for its extensive love and care in making quality vinegars.

VINEGARS, WINE – See above!

DRY AND PACAKAGED GOODS

ARBORIO RICE – glutinous, short-grained rice used for making risotto—also good for rice puddings.

BREAD CRUMBS – an Italian staple, plain or seasoned.

CANNED TOMATOES, SAN MARZANO – a special heirloom variety tomato, used for making sauces.

GNOCCHI – potato dumplings, fresh in shelf stable packaging or frozen. They're tricky to make from scratch, but the ready-made type are easy and delicious, and go with just about every pasta sauce.

PASTA, DRY OR FRESH – See p. 85 for artisan-made pastas of St. Louis.

PIZELLES – thin, intricately-patterned, sometimes anise-flavored dessert wafers that go well with ice cream

PIZZA CRUSTS – available fresh, frozen, and sometimes still as a blob of dough.

POLENTA – ground cornmeal, dry and uncooked, or premade and ready to serve. Top with tomato sauce, serve with meat or fish.

ROASTED PEPPERS – sold in jars or cans with oil.

SUN-DRIED TOMATOES – a sweet addition to pastas.

MISCELLANY

ANCHOVIES, WHITE – packed in olive oil.

BISCOTTI – a dense, subtly sweet cookie usually served with coffee.

CHESNUT HONEY – a dark and delicious nectar used for sweet or savory dishes; a Tuscan delight made by bees feeding from chestnut trees.

OLIVES – Kalamata, Sicilian, Picholine, Alfonso, Gaeta, Taggiasca, Cerignola, and many delicious others.

TOASTED RAVIOLI – a beloved St. Louis tradition, usually found frozen and ready to fry or bake. Serve with marinara on the side for dipping.

TRUFFLES – extremely pungent and expensive mushrooms. Find them dried, canned, or infused in oil.

NOTES ON INGREDIENTS AND PRODUCTS

_____

_____

_____

_____

_____

_____

_____

STORES

DIGREGORIO'S
5200 Daggett Ave.
The Hill
314/776-1062

DiGregorio's is simply my favorite Italian grocery. It is well-lit, spacious, and full of Italian treasures, including the quiet older lady who works the counter and barely knows any English. (Don't worry, there are plenty of English-speaking employees roaming the floor and behind the deli counter.)

The deli counter may be the most exciting part of DiGregorio's. It's stocked full of soft and pungent cheeses and salty, rich salamis—all of which will be happily sliced to order, plus ready-to-cook _salsiccia_, freshly ground pork sausage bursting with fennel and black pepper. For your next brunch Bloody Marys, create something wowing from their selection of giant green and black olives, spicy pickled peperocinis, zingy marinated cheese-stuffed roasted peppers, and the zippy cauliflower from a jar of hot giardinera.

It's too bad there's no produce, but DiGregorio's makes up for it with wine and liquor. Fill your cart with Italian vino like Chiantis, Verdicchios, Primativos, and Super Tuscans, or specialty liqueurs like Limoncello and the love-it-or-hate-it Grappa.

You'll find plenty of dry pastas and housemade sauces to stock your pantry for those "I just wanna make spaghetti" kind of days. There are bulk spices and a selection of oils and vinegars for the days you feel more like really cooking. And, DiGregorio's carries the treats you buy when having guests over, like amaretto cookies, ladyfingers, pizelles, and the Jordan almonds my grandma always had out for Christmas.

Finally, add DiGregorio's to your go-to-for-gifts list (you've started one by this far in the book, right?). Surely someone you know—perhaps yourself!—needs decorative Italianate plates, aprons with pictures of pasta, tablecloths trimmed with fruit patterns, whimsical ceramic figurines, fancy oil dispensers, and exquisite gadgets like gnocchi boards, wooden spoons, and ravioli makers.

PICCOLINO'S ITALIAN GROCER
piccolinosfoodandwine.com
10 Church St.
Ferguson
314/942-2255

A surprising find in the middle of Old Town Ferguson, Piccolino's is a brand new Italian grocery right across from the famous Whistle Stop (an old train depot now a restaurant and ice cream/custard shop). My first thought upon discovery was that I was just plain happy to find a new, and another, small grocery in North St. Louis.

It's a small place—even the name means cute and tiny—but bright, clean, and inviting. Piccolino's offers all the typical St. Louis Italian fare: canned artichoke hearts, fresh breadcrumbs, olive oil, canned tomatoes, dried pasta, and a selection of wines. A small deli case contains a spread of Boar's Head deli meats and all types of cheeses, and they make sandwiches (meatball, salsiccia, muffaleta) to order. Brewed coffee is always available, and I avail myself of that, especially on snowy, winter days.

The owner said a very promising thing to me after I eyed the local fresh pasta in the cooler, "We are really trying to focus on selling local products here." Cheers to that.

URZI'S ITALIAN MARKET
5430 Southwest Ave.
The Hill
314/645-3914

Urzi's is a bit off The Hill's main drag, but hits all the marks of a classic Italian grocery. On Southwest Avenue near historic Hanneke Hardware and Cunetto's House of Pasta, Urzi's has two small storefronts jam packed with Italian treats. The aisles are full and do seem to change a bit with the seasons, but you will always find nuts and dried fruits (many of them covered in chocolate), almond paste, Italian candies, canned tomatoes, artichoke hearts, anchovies of various types, bread crumbs, frozen pizza, and pints of gelato. Don't miss the huge selection of Italian wines and liqueurs, or the amazing selection of extracts, including Oil of Bitter Almond (if you feel like kicking your boring almond extract to the curb), great for baking. Like most Italian Groceries, Urzi's whole spice selection is impressive and easy on the wallet.

Speaking of affordable…they have a soon-to-be-your-favorite Olive Oil Packed Tuna for just under $3. This fish is worlds away from the watery and stinky, fishy stuff we're used to—delicate and with the taste of actual tuna. I love tossing this into pasta with garlic, olives, and good quality oil, or making it the centerpiece of a superb salad niçoise.

Among the different cooking utensils and cookware, is a notable selection of Moka Pots—a cooktop version of an espresso machine, that is much cheaper and more functional than the giant countertop contraption most people end up buying. On the shelves next to the pots are pounds and pounds of coffee, of all different roasts.

Last, but certainly not least, Urzi's makes their own fresh sausages, including salciccia and *luganiga* (mildly spiced pork sausage), which they offer alongside all kinds of salami and other cured meats.

VIVIANO AND SONS GROCERS
shopviviano.com
5139 Shaw Ave.
The Hill
314/771-5476

Right around the corner from DiGregorio's, you can find another little Italian market loaded with character and wonderful food and imports, the famous Viviano and Sons. The generations of family portraits on the wall behind the checkout counter chronicle the history of the Viviano family, this store, and St. Louis Italians—authenticity, nostalgia, and a good history lesson!

My favorite part of this neighborhood store are the huge buckets of olives in the middle of the store. In its very rustic way, it harkens back to the rural Italian roots of the immigrants that built The Hill. Barrels hold all sorts, pitted, stuffed, or au naturel: shiny, dried, black, marinated Sicilian, big round and green, the ever popular kalamatas. Look for their very popular colorful green olive salad sold alongside sandwiches and salads at the deli counter.

You can expect all the Italian staples: great cheeses, breadcrumbs, jugs of olive oil, almond cookies, vinegars, and family. Share the family love by taking something home from their large cheese selection, or buy a big bag of handmade, stuffed frozen pasta to feed your hungry troops. There are racks of large containers of affordable spices and dried herbs, along with ever-present cans of tomatoes, tins of anchovies, dried mushrooms, and marinated artichoke hearts. They also have wine and liquor, a few housemade sauces, and a small library of books about The Hill.

Vivano's is surely the center of one of the U.S.'s great Italian American communities. Go in and be inspired.

VIVIANO FESTA ITALIANO MARKET
62 Fenton Plz.
Fenton
636/305-1474

150 Four Seasons Plz.
Chesterfield
314/878-1474

These two markets are related to, but not affiliated with, the Viviano's market on The Hill. The Viviano Markets in Fenton and Chesterfield include full service deli counters that serve pastas, salads, sandwiches, and desserts. Get Boar's Head deli meats, Volpi salamis, imported prosciutto, and Italian cheeses sliced for you to take home along with a pound of briny olives.

The places stock tons of different shapes of dry pasta (fusili, anelletti, strascinati, ditali, tubetti, ziti, and more), lots of canned tomatoes, and house-labeled pasta sauces. You're not likely to, but don't miss the wine and spice sections. Or the freezers, stocked with meat and cheese stuffed ravioli and tortellini, and housemade and ready-to-cook lasagna. For authentic Italian after-dinner offerings, they have pizelles, biscotti, and amaretti. Freshly made tiramisu works too!

The only difference between these plaza outlets and the markets on The Hill are the lack of items geared towards first generation Italian immigrants. But that doesn't keep them from being excellent places to shop.

VOLPI ITALIAN SALAMI & MEAT COMPANY
volpifoods.com
5263 Northrup Ave.
The Hill
314/772-8550
See entry on p. 60.

NOTES ON ITALIAN STORES

_____
_____
_____
_____
_____
_____

RECIPES

MY GRANDMA'S MEATBALL RECIPE

2 lbs ground beef
1 egg
$^1/_3$ c bread crumbs (preferably the seasoned Italian type)
salt and pepper to taste

1 medium onion, chopped
1 small can tomato paste
2 cloves garlic, minced
2 small cans plain tomato sauce
1 T dry oregano
1 T dry basil
salt and pepper to taste

- Mix ground beef, egg, bread crumbs, and salt and pepper to taste in a bowl until thoroughly mixed.
- Roll into small (approx. 2-ounce) meatballs and set aside.
- Sauté onion in a deep sauté pan with a fitted lid.
- Once soft and translucent, add tomato paste.
- Stir to spread paste evenly.
- Add garlic, tomato sauce, herbs, and salt and pepper to taste. Stir until smooth.
- Add raw meatballs to pan so that they're just covering the bottom in one layer. You will probably have to make them in batches.
- Put the lid on and cook the meatballs on medium heat until they're done through, flipping meatballs once they're cooked on the bottom.
- Enjoy! These are the most flavorful and moist meatballs I've ever eaten.

MUSHROOM RISOTTO CAKES | MAKES 10 CAKES

Mushrooms
2 c dried wild mushrooms, such as porcinis, shiitakes, and/or morels
3 T olive oil
1 c shallots, peeled and thinly sliced
2 cloves garlic, peeled
6 c chicken stock
2 c dry red wine
2 c dry white wine
2 sprigs fresh thyme
1 t sugar
1 T kosher salt
2 t white pepper

Risotto
2 T olive oil
½ c yellow onion, chopped
3 c Arborio rice
reserved mushroom liquid from previous step
reserved chopped mushrooms from previous step
½ stick unsalted butter, softened
3 T dry vermouth
1 c grated parmesan, Asiago, or fontina cheese, or a combination
1 T truffle oil

First, prepare the mushrooms.
- Soak dried mushrooms in water overnight in the refrigerator. Drain thoroughly before cooking.
- Heat olive oil in large saucepan.
- Add shallots and garlic, and sauté until caramelized, about 3 to 5 minutes. (If you're using fresh mushrooms, this would be the time to add them, and sauté until soft.)
- Add dried mushrooms and all remaining ingredients to shallot mixture Bring to boil.
- Boil 10 minutes, then strain through fine sieve, reserving liquid.
- Remove thyme sprigs from solids.
- Transfer solids to food processor, and pulse to chop. Set aside.
- Pour reserved mushroom liquid into a large pot. Bring to a boil.
- Reduce heat, and simmer to keep warm.

Then, on to the risotto.
- In a large, heavy saucepan, heat olive oil over medium heat.
- Sauté onions, stirring occasionally, until soft and translucent, about 4 to 5 minutes.
- Add rice and stir 2 to 3 minutes, until grains are completely coated with oil.
- Increase heat to medium-high. Stir in 2 c warm reserved mushroom liquid.
- Using wooden spoon, stir mixture continuously, being careful to scrape up all rice from bottom of saucepan.
- When liquid has been absorbed, repeat previous step, adding 2 c mushroom liquid.
- Continue with remaining mushroom stock until rice is soft and all liquid is absorbed.
- If reserved liquid runs out before rice reaches desired consistency, use hot water in small amounts.
- Once risotto has reached desired consistency, add reserved chopped mushrooms, butter, and vermouth. Stir to combine.
- Remove saucepan from heat, and stir in cheese and truffle oil.
- Spread risotto into thin, even layer on rimmed baking sheet. Set aside to cool.

Finish the cakes.
- Heat oven to 450°.
- Form risotto into small cakes, and place on baking sheet either greased or lined with parchment paper.
- Bake cakes until they start to become crisp, about 15 minutes.
- Serve as the main course or a side. Great with meat, fish, or salad.

CITRUS ROSEMARY MARINATED OLIVES

1½ c black olives
1½ c green olives
3 T extra virgin olive oil
1 t red pepper flakes
juice and zest from one lemon
juice and zest from one-half orange
1 clove garlic, crushed
2–3 sprigs of rosemary, chopped

- Toss all ingredients in a bowl.
- Eat immediately. Or, keep in the fridge for up to one week.

INDIA AND PAKISTAN

The cuisines of India and Pakistan are diverse, shaped by varying geographies and fascinating histories, and guided by the dietary restrictions of the four predominant religions: Hinduism (vegetarian or no beef), Islam (no pork), Buddhism (vegetarian), and Sikhism (vegetarian). These spice-driven cuisines can also be hard to pin down as they have changed frequently over time due to their contact with other cultures, as well as the predilection for passing recipes down orally and proclaiming that the ways of one's family or village are, really, the real way of doing it. There are hundreds of types of curry alone (read more about curry on p. 197).

The food in the north of India has been heavily influenced by the Mediterranean (remember the Spice Trade?) as well as the invasion of the Mongols in the eleventh century. Here you'll find lamb, chicken, and goat dishes, along with ample use of yogurt, cream, and curries. The south is predominantly vegetarian, and reflects a more Asian influence. There's a greater emphasis on lime, coconut, spice blends, and, again, curries. Chutneys play a huge role in all Indian meals, adding bright tangy flavors to the table.

These cuisines are truly a melting pot of foods. Traversed, explored, invaded, and visited by land and sea by many cultures over the centuries, those from other lands have introduced new foods that are now an integral part of eating on the Indian subcontinent: chilies and potatoes from the Portuguese, tea from the British, and cashews and almonds from Persia, to name a few.

INGREDIENTS AND PRODUCTS

It's true for most of the ethnic foodstuffs covered in this book, but particularly those found in Indian groceries: please note that spellings may vary widely for all sorts of practical, cultural, and lost-in-translation reasons.

MEAT

HALAL MEATS – halal is to Islam, as kosher is to Judaism. The meat is raised, slaughtered, and prepared according to Muslim dietary laws.

CHEESE AND DAIRY

DHAI – yogurt. Indians often top salads, sides, or dal with yogurt for a creamy garnish.

GHEE – long-cooked, shelf-stable clarified butter, with a delicious nutty flavor and a high smoke point, and great for sautéing. All these things makes ghee more versatile than traditional butter—and some claim it's healthier for you.

KULFI – ice cream made with heavy cream and sweetened condensed milk, in flavors like mango, pistachio, or saffron. Not to be missed.

PANEER – fresh cow's milk cheese, curdled with lime or lemon juice, and pressed until firm, often used with cooked peas, spinach, or other greens. It has a very subtle, sweet flavor and can be used in much the same way as tofu.

PRODUCE

CAULIFLOWER

EGGPLANT

GREEN CHILIES

KARELA – bitter melon, a vegetable with bumpy green skins and a crunchy texture. Salt and rinse before putting in stir fries or soups to relieve some of the bitterness.

MANGOES – many different varieties, but all are soft when ripe and candy sweet.

OKRA

TINDORA – ivy gourd, a flexible little vegetable, good for soups, curries, stir fries, pickles, and salads.

SPICES

Just a small sampling of what's used and what's available.

AMCHOOR – a sour and fragrant powder made from dried green (unripe) mangoes.

CARDAMOM – green, white, or black; ground seeds, whole seeds, or whole pods.

CUMIN

DHANIA – coriander powder.

HALDI – turmeric.

HING – asafetida, a pungent spice used to flavor pickles, curries, and sprinkled on naan.

KALA JEERA – black cumin.

KALONJI – nigella, black onion seeds.

METHI – fenugreek powder.

MUSTARD SEED

NUTMEG

SAFFRON – a bright orange/red spice and one of the most expensive, saffron is used mostly to flavor rice or in sauces accompanying seafood.

SESAME SEEDS – raw or toasted, they add a wonderful texture and flavor to food. Black and white varieties commonly available.

SPICE BLENDS AND CONDIMENTS

CHUTNEY – a condiment made of vegetables, fruit, or herbs, crushed with spices and vinegar. Sweet, spicy, or sweet and spicy, top Indian breads or snacks (or your morning toast) with chutney.

CURRY – available in paste or powder (see sidebar on p. 197).

PICKLES – a staple in the Indian diet, you can find just about anything pickled, including mangoes, lemons, limes, cauliflower, tomatoes, pumpkin, eggplant, okra, and carrots.

MASALA – like curry, a blend of spices; the types are numerous and varied.

BREADS AND SNACKS

CHAAT (OR INGREDIENTS FOR MAKING) – a uniquely Indian snack with a base of fried dough/dough pieces and add-ons like potatoes, chickpeas, crispy cereals or noodle pieces, chutney(s), spice mixes, coriander leaves, yogurt, and then some.

NAAN, NAN – round, flat, often buttery bread baked until soft, fluffy, and delicious. Buy frozen or fresh, and eat with spicy foods and/or more butter.

NAMKEEN – delicious fried snacks or snack mixes, sweet, salty, and/or spicy, in more varieties and shapes than you can imagine, and eaten between meals or with tea.

PAPADUM, PAPAD – round, thin, crispy cracker-like bread usually made with black gram, lentil, or chickpea flour and seasoned with things like black pepper, cumin, or chilies.

PARATHA – whole wheat, pan-fried flat bread, often stuffed with potatoes, cauliflower, radishes, or paneer.

PURI, POORI – small, circular, deep-fried unleavened bread eaten mostly as a snack.

DRY AND PACKAGED GOODS

DAL – dried lentils, peas, and beans that have been hulled and split, meaning they cook quickly and create their own thick broth in the cooking process. A staple of Indian eating. I love to throw them into soups or stews.

FLOURS – a bounty of flours, many non-wheat, and most unknown to American cooks:

- ladu, laddu, ladoo flour – a special combination of chickpea, wheat, and coconut flours used to make a favorite dessert (ladoos).
- dhokra flour – rice and chickpea flour.
- moong flour – mung bean flour.
- rajgara (rajgira) flour – amaranth flour.
- ragi (bajri) flour – millet flour.
- besan flour – chickpea flour.
- mathia flour – a flour made of peas and lentils.
- matpe flour – a lentil flour used for making papadum.

WHAT IS CURRY ANYWAY?

Curry literally means "gravy," and it's simply a name applied to a spice blend used to flavor a side dish of meat and/or vegetables, with a gravy-like consistency. This gravy is served with a grain, generally rice, or freshly made bread (Indians often make fresh breads at every meal that go straight from the stovetop or special griddle to the tabletop). These starches are considered the main event of the meal. Many countries in Asia have curries, and each one is vastly different from the rest. Some are blended with coconut milk, while others are blended with yogurt.

Indian curry is typically comprised of coriander, cumin, mustard, black pepper, fenugreek, and turmeric, with many, many variations spinning off from there. Curries can be made with vegetables or meats, or simply be a sauce. With no definitive recipe for this spicy dish, it begs for your experimentation—go for it!

NOTES ON INGREDIENTS AND PRODUCTS

STORES

AKBAR
10606 Page Ave.
Olivette
314/428-1900

Akbar does two things extremely well: It boasts the best fresh halal meat selection around town, and the spices to cook them in.

You will find about only three aisles, all of which are mostly filled with spices. Make your own intoxicating curry, chai spice, or rub with such things as *haldi* (ground turmeric), *methi* (fenugreek powder), *dhania* (coriander powder), coriander seeds, white pepper, black pepper, paprika, poppy seeds, ajwain seeds (smell like thyme, but more pungent), and cumin seeds and powder. There's also *khejur gur*, a.k.a jaggery, the sugar from the date palm tree.

At Akbar's butcher counter, find whole lamb, as well as cut-up pieces if you don't think that will fit in your oven. You can buy whole turkeys, chickens, and Cornish hens. Imagine a Cornish hen rubbed with curry spices, served with sautéed tindora (see p. 202) and fluffy basmati rice. Dig through a freezer full of catfish, king fish, salmon, *hilsha* (the oily, tropical ilish), and more with colloquial names I couldn't get transalted (but I'm excited to take them all home and try them anyhow!).

AKSHAR FOODS
aksharfoods.com
12419 St. Charles Rock Rd.
Bridgeton
314/291-6666

Set back from the road, this square building houses one of the biggest and most extensive Indian and Pakistani food emporiums in the St. Louis region, offering up a wide variety of rice, dal, lentils, flours, sweets, and even home decorations, and boasting super fresh produce. Expect the expected potatoes, onions, tindora, mangoes, eggplant, and ginger alongside some interesting (*kantola* or spiny gourd—usually peeled of its spiny skin and pickled or curried) and surprising items (fresh dates—can be eaten right off the branch, they get sweeter as they ripen from golden yellow to brown). Their spice section, especially if you are looking for large quantities, is a must see for things like big bags of sesame seeds, whole cloves, green pods of cardamom, whole or ground cumin, or black and yellow mustard seeds (try in the Madras Potatoes Recipe on p. 119). With bags of spices this big and cheap, you can't afford not to try your hand at making fresh curry.

One of my favorite sights at this place is the row of jaggery blocks wrapped in burlap and tied with string. Jaggery is unfiltered date, palm, or cane sugar—basically a version of sugar in the raw—and is a secret ingredient in curry, dal, and just about all Indian sweets. It is a good idea when using jaggery to strain it yourself: Shave pieces from the block and place in pan with some water (enough to wet the sugar), turn on medium heat and warm until melted, then put through a mesh strainer to get out any impurities. Once you've done this, reduce the sugar to a syrupy consistency and it's ready to use in a recipe.

Akshar serves food seven days a week, things like heaping plates of chaat; fried and salty snacks like samosas, papads, and puri; sandwiches; biryani; curries; dal; and pav bhaji from their colorfully decorated food counter. Places like Akshar makes grocery shopping fun again.

MID-EAST MARKET
14345 Manchester Rd.
Ballwin
636/230-7018

The name of Mid-East Market is a little off target: With items like jaggery (date plam sugar) and masala (the remarkable spice mix) dominating its wares, it most certainly seems more like an Indian store.

The outside of this strip mall store lures you in with pictures of roasted chicken, rice, kebabs, and pizza. Though I didn't find pizza, they do have wonderful prepared foods, starting with hands-down the best grocery store samosas I have ever had—warm, filled with spiced potatoes and peas, and only a dollar. You can also grab a beautifully roasted chicken—ready to go—and some freshly made *gulab jamun* (Indian sweet cheese dumplings spiced with cardamom, rosewater, and saffron) or a *jilawii/jalebi* (Indian donuts, fried and dipped in a sugar syrup spiced with rosewater) for dessert. I've never tried their halal tacos, but I'm sure that would be one thing to write home about.

Once you've snacked, you can get back to groceries! The butcher counter advertises *zabiha*, which is the Arabic word for halal, and has an extremely extensive meat menu. The super clean cutting area was full of freshly broken down goat—you can buy just about every piece, from the brain, shoulder, chops, and ribs, to the liver, legs, and kidneys. (If you really want to have a party, you can buy one whole!) If goat doesn't, well, get your goat, they have beef including brain, oxtail, tripe, and tongue; veal; chicken; and even duckling. Lamb was the selling point for me—at between $4.99 and $6.99 a pound, it's a steal.

Traditional Indian vegetables (bitter melon, *tindora*, eggplant, okra) and culinary staples (onion, carrots, and potatoes) beckon from the produce section, as do small containers of fresh peeled garlic. Imagine not having to peel those twenty cloves of garlic for your next pasta sauce, and always having a clove ready and waiting to throw in with your sautéed vegetables.

Finally, you can't leave any Indian store (even if it is Middle Eastern) without checking out their spice section and grabbing a few premade curries.

SEEMA ENTERPRISES
14238 Manchester Rd.
Manchester
636/391-5914

Walk into Seema and a mountain of rice greets you. Bags and bags of different kinds of jasmine, basmati, matta (red rice, popular in Sri Lanka, that plumps well and has an earthy flavor), and dubraj (aromatic, short-grain) rices, each one a little different from the next. Break out of the plain white rice rut, and venture on to the mountain.

My very favorite thing about this location of Seema are the desserts I've rarely seen elsewhere in St. Louis. They have *barfi*, hovering in its deliciousness somewhere between cheesecake and fudge, and made of milk, ghee, and usually flavored with cardamom powder. You can find it plain, *pista* (green with pistachios), tri-color, cashew, black *jamun* (plum), or almond. These sweet creamy and/or gritty treats melt in your mouth when you eat them. I suggest getting one of each (but pista is certainly my favorite). They also have little yellow squares of *cham cham*, a Bengali sweet of flour, cream, and lemon, scented with saffron. Or, or, or…Try the similar *kalakand*, a sweet made of sweet milk and cottage cheese, or *peda*, made from sweet milk and Indian ricotta (called *khoa*).

This place has a delightful thing I've never seen in another Indian shop, herbs chopped and frozen into ice cube-like blocks for easy use. They have fenugreek, *palak* (spinach), coriander (cilantro), and others ready to be plunked into *dal*, a curry, or a simple afternoon soup.

There's more! They have, most awesomely, chopped and frozen vegetables hard to find elsewhere—*tindora* (ivy gourd), *kantola* (spiny gourd), *karela* (bitter melon), okra, and *suran* (yam). Bored with corn and peas? These will make interesting replacements in your next stew or chili. Seema also has a huge selection of papads, thin wafer-like cracker breads made from *urad* (black lentil) flour and cumin, and available in tons of flavors. Eat with chutneys for a great snack!

You will also find the staples of any Indian grocery here, shelves and shelves of spices and curry mixes, bags of lentils and beans, those unexpected flours, fresh paneer, and piles of produce.

SEEMA ENTERPRISES & SEEMA WORLD TRAVEL
10635 Page Ave.
Olivette
314/423 -9990

Seema is basically across the street from Akbar (see p. 197) on Page Avenue, so you can plan on visiting both with the same trip. This store is one of my favorites, and that could very well be because the man behind the counter is so friendly and helpful. Or, it could be the astonishing selection of just about anything and everything Indian, including a mesmerizing number of spices.

The produce has its own little room by the door, with crates and tables of cucumbers, *dosakai* (yellow Indian cucumbers), plantains, onions, potatoes, spinach, okra, tomatoes, *tindora* (ivy gourd), *karela* (bitter melon), guvar beans (the source of guar gum), and other traditional ingredients. Don't be afraid to experiment, or just try one of the recipes I have included on p. 202–204.

The freezer is stocked with *kulfi* (ice cream), as well as lots of frozen entrées and appetizers. Their dry goods include many different types of lentils and beans, rice and flours, chutneys and pickles, oils and curries, instant meals, and jaggery (date palm sugar). They have lots of different types of fresh breads, including naan, paratha, pita, and papadum, and all in many different flavors. Trade out your olive oil for a can of ghee, or feed your family oven baked samosas instead of pizza rolls (samosas actually have vegetables in them!).

There is a large section of an Indian favorite, mouth fresheners, mixtures chewed or eaten after dinner to cleanse the palate and aid digestion. You can find *anardana goli*, made of pomegranate seeds; *mukhwaas*, made of fennel seeds, anise seeds, coconut, and sesame seeds, tossed in sugar and peppermint oil; *abajpati goli*, marble-sized candies made of cumin, coriander, black pepper, cloves, ginger, and cinnamon; or just plain cardamom pods.

Seema Enterprises is an extremely hospitable place to shop, and besides, they always seem have what I'm looking for, and plenty of other things to inspire me.

NOTES ON INDIAN AND PAKISTANI STORES

RECIPES

SAUTÉED TINDORA | SERVES 4 AS A SIDE DISH

1 t cumin seeds
1 T oil
2 c tindora, quartered, longways, about a pound
pinch cayenne
½ t garam masala (optional)
juice of half a lime

- Toast cumin in a dry pan, about one minute. You will know it's done when the aroma of cumin hits your nose.
- Add oil, tindora, and cayenne (you can use red pepper flakes instead).
- Sauté until the tindora is browned, but still has a crunch to it.
- Add lime juice and garam masala.
- Remove from heat and serve.
- Served as a side with rice, and stewed lamb or a simple roasted chicken (see p. 133).

SWEET POTATO STUFFED MINI SAMOSAS | SERVES 8–10

Feel free to freeze after assembly, then pop them frozen into the oven for 10 to 15 minutes to heat.

[NOTE: see instructional video on ShopLikeaChef.com]

Filling

1 medium sweet potato, peeled and diced
2 carrots, peeled and diced
1 small onion, diced
3 cloves garlic, minced
1 T oil
2 t curry powder
splash of water

Dough

1lb all-purpose flour
4 t salt
4 T vegetable oil
6 oz warm water

First, make the filling.
- Sauté onions, garlic, and curry powder in oil until soft. Add potato and carrots.
- Turn heat to low, add water, and cover.
- Cook until vegetables are soft.

Then, make the dough.
- Mix flour and salt in bowl.
- Make a well in the center of the dough, and add oil and water. (You might want to start with ½ of the water, and add it slowly if you need it.)
- Knead the dough until it's soft.
- Set aside, covered, for about 30 minutes to rest.
- Divide the dough into 12 equal pieces.
- Roll pieces out into circles. Cut the circles in half.
- Brush the flat edge with water and form a cone around your finger, sealing the dampened edge.

Finally, assemble and cook.
- Fill with filling and press the open edge together. Place on a cookie sheet.
- Bake in a preheated oven at 350°, for 10 to 15 minutes, until golden brown. (Or, if you're feeling extremely inspired, you can fry them in a few inches of oil.)
- Serve with chutney, perhaps the arugula chutney recipe below.

ARUGULA CHUTNEY

1 lb fresh arugula
juice from 3 limes
3 T olive oil

- Place everything into a food processor, and process until smooth.
- Lasts about a week in the fridge.
- Use like any chutney, or serve with the samosas (prior recipe).

ALMOND KHEER (ALMOND RICE PUDDING)

¾ c basmati rice
1½ c water
4 c almond milk
½–¾ c sugar
1–2 t vanilla extract
½ c almonds and cashew nuts chopped (you can use one or the other)
2 T golden raisins
¾ t cardamom powder, or the seeds from about 10 pods, crushed
1 T canola oil

- Heat the rice and the water until they come to a boil.
- Lower the heat, cover, and simmer for about 10 to 15 minutes until the water is absorbed by the rice.
- Add to this the almond milk, vanilla, and ½ to ¾ c sugar, depending on how sweet you want it to be.
- Let the kheer simmer for about 45 minutes, stirring occasionally until it has thickened.
- Let it remain a little fluid because it will thicken as it stands.
- Heat the oil in a small skillet.
- Add the nuts, and stir until lightly browned.
- Add the raisins and cardamom powder, and stir for about a minute.
- Pour these things on top the kheer for decoration.
- Serve warm or chilled.

CHINA, KOREA, AND SOUTHEAST ASIA

As a general rule, Asian cuisines are based on balance—a mixture of color, texture, temperature, sweetness, and sourness. To lump all of the Asian cuisines together is doing each one a huge disservice, as they're all uniquely delicious and interesting. I could spend all day talking about the virtues of each one but don't worry, I won't. They're lumped together here because you will find their ingredients and products sold side by side in a handful of specialty St. Louis groceries—that is the logic of commerce in a foreign, melting pot country, which may not line up with culinary, cultural, or geographical distinctions elsewhere.

Most of the groceries listed below could probably also fit into the *Multiethnic Stores* chapter (see p. 220) because very few of them actually carry products from only one Asian county. Some even carry European or North and Central American products.

THE ASIAN CUISINES OF ST. LOUIS

There are close to twenty countries in East Asia (formerly "The Far East") and Southeast Asia, but I want to highlight the four major cultures represented in St. Louis.

CHINESE – With at least eight distinct regional cuisines, the food of China alone is wide-ranging and hard to sum up, but I can start by listing some major flavors and ingredients: mushrooms, garlic, ginger, soy sauce, sesame oil, rice vinegar, shrimp paste, chilies, peanuts, and citrus.

KOREAN – Korean food is distinctive and less varied, centered mostly around seafood soups and stews, cooked in clay pots, and almost always accompanied by kimchee (a popular condiment and side dish of fermented vegetables). It's also known for its BBQ, usually thinly-sliced beef sirloin or marinated short ribs. Ginger, fish sauce, soy sauce, rice vinegar, chilies, and garlic are the main seasonings.

THAI – Thai cuisine has a large Indian influence, which is why there are so many pungent Thai curries. These include yellow (based on roasted spices, usually turmeric with the addition of a little cayenne for heat), red (made of mature and dried red chilies), and green (made from young green chilies, which have a more concentrated heat than mature red ones), all of which have a coconut milk base. Thai cooking is light, with fresh ingredients that are cooked quickly or steamed. Lemongrass, coconut milk, cilantro, cumin, garlic, chilies, peanuts, and basil predominate.

VIETNAMESE – Vietnam was a French colony for about fifty years, which definitely left is imprint on the Mongol/Chinese-based cuisine. Vietnamese cuisine is also light, centered around crepes, baguette sandwiches, clear broths, and fresh herbs, and redolent of limes, mint, ginger, lemongrass, basil, garlic, and coriander.

INGREDIENTS AND PRODUCTS

MEAT

BACON, CHINESE – air-cured bacon made with brown sugar, soy sauce, and spices.

BEEF – thinly sliced sirloin, skirt steak, and flank steak, as well as ground beef.

CHICKEN, FEET AND ALL – found fresh and frozen.

DUCK, WHOLE

LAP CHANG – Chinese smoked, dried pork sausage.

PORK – from snout to tail, in many forms.

SHORT RIBS, KOREAN – thin sliced, bone-in beef ribs.

FISH AND SEAFOOD

FISH – tilapia, cod, snapper, grouper, smelt, pike, and catfish.

GEODUCKS – huge mollusks native to the Pacific Northwest of the U.S. that have become an extremely popular Asian ingredient.

MUSSELS AND LITTLE NECK CLAMS – available fresh and frozen, these are great for soups. Or, steam them with lemongrass and ginger.

PERIWINKLES – edible sea snails. Boil in salted water and eat with soy sauce, or add to a stir fry with chili sauce.

SHRIMP – available fresh and frozen.

PRODUCE

BITTER MELONS – See. p. 194.

BOK CHOY, REGULAR AND BABY – "Chinese cabbage," this crisp and sweet leafy vegetable can be steamed or added to a stir fry.

CHESTNUTS – favorite Asian nuts, sold fresh when in season, eaten boiled or roasted.

DAIKONS – white Japanese radishes that can be used as any radish would. The flavor is a little milder than the little red cousins that we know.

EGGPLANTS – many varieties, like Japanese (purple, long, and slender), Black Beauty (dark and oval), Thai green (green, long, and slender), and many with striped skins, but they all taste similar.

GAI LAN – "Chinese broccoli," this long and slender veggie with slick leaves and small flower heads, is similar in flavor to broccoli, but a bit sweeter. Use anywhere you use broccoli, even the thick stem.

GINGER – one of the most well-known Asian ingredients, a very flavorful and biting rhizome. Peel and add to soups, stews, teas, stir fries, and juices (excellent for soothing indigestion).

KUMQUATS – tiny citrus fruits that look like oranges, but are about the size and shape of large olives. Eat them raw, rind and all. The rind is sweet and the pulp is sour.

LEMONGRASS – a long, woody, and *inedible* herb, but it is smashed with the butt of a knife (to release the oils) and added to soups and stews, for a bright, delicious, fragrant effect.

LONG BEANS – measuring about a foot and a half, these beans are long, and are close to green beans in flavor. Eat them raw or cooked.

LOTUS ROOT – a beautiful addition to salads (should be lightly boiled first to retain it color and crunch) or stir fries. Peel and slice thin to use.

LYCHEES – mostly available in cans, packed in syrup, but you can buy them fresh, with thin pink skins, only once a year. Be sure to grab a pack when you see them, and you won't be disappointed.

MANGOSTEENS – fruit with purple skins and sweet flesh.

NAPA CABBAGE – a type of Chinese cabbage (see also bok choy above) that's crisp and light, great for a coleslaw or an addition to a salad.

PEA SHOOTS – the tender vines and leaves of pea plants, which can be eaten raw in salad or lightly sautéed. They have a great pea taste and a lovely crunchy texture.

SPICES, SAUCES, AND CONDIMENTS

CHILI-GARLIC PASTE – made of just these two ingredients, a perfect spicy condiment.

COCONUT MILK – sold in cans, this is a typical ingredient in Thai curries, but it's also used for soups (like the Thai *tom kha* soup) and rice dishes.

CURRY PASTES – found in cans and as powders in more varieties than I can keep track of.

FISH SAUCE – an important seasoning for many Asian dishes, this sauce has a very concentrated fish flavor (and a slightly offensive smell), but if used sparingly it can add incredible depth to your food.

HOISIN SAUCE – a sweet and spicy Chinese sauce that's a great fit for chicken, beef, and pork.

KIMCHEE – a Korean staple (and national dish) made of spicy fermented vegetables, eaten mostly as a side dish. Sold in jars, most have a base vegetable like cabbage or radish, but some versions may have fish or seafood.

MISO – Japanese fermented soy bean paste used as a flavoring or soup base. Common types include *shiro* (white), *aka* (red), *awase* (red and white), and *koshi* (strained).

OYSTER SAUCE – traditionally made from reduced oyster extracts, the more modern versions of this classic sauce contain thickening agents, salt, and preservatives. Use to flavor stir fries or steamed vegetables.

OYSTER SAUCE, VEGETARIAN – made from mushrooms, and tastes close to the original.

PLUM SAUCE – a sweet and sour Chinese dipping sauce used mostly with spring rolls and other fried items.

SESAME OIL – a delicious addition to a vinaigrette or stir fry, you can find this oil infused with any number of things, including chilies, ginger, and lemongrass. It's very pungent and a little goes a long way—take it drop by drop.

SHRIMP PASTE – made of fermented ground shrimp, this paste has an extremely strong flavor, so use restraint when doling it out for additional flavor to soups, stews, and stir fries.

SOY SAUCE – likely the best known Asian condiment, you can find it in original, low sodium, and the thick aged type. Each culture makes its own slightly different soy sauce, all worthy of exploration.

SRIRACHA SAUCE – A bright red spicy condiment/hot sauce named for the town of Si Racha in Thailand made of chilies, vinegar, and garlic. It's also known as "Rooster Sauce" because the most common American version (made by Huy Fong Foods of California) has a big rooster on the front of the bottle. Sure you use it to add extra heat to Thai and Vietnamese dishes, but this chili-garlic sauce with a slightly sweet taste works on almost anything from eggs to hot dogs.

DRY AND PACKAGED GOODS

NOODLES – rice and buckwheat noodles (soba) are most popular. Though the widths and shapes differ (square, round, flat), they're all long and cook rather quickly.

NORI – seaweed used to wrap sushi. It's also roasted and eaten as a snack, and a good addition to soups.

PANKO – Japanese bread crumbs. They're light, flaky, and a great alternative to conventional crumbs. The secret of their popular fluffiness is that they're not actually made from bread, but from a flour paste that's spread over bamboo mats to dry.

RICE – rice comes in more varieties than most of us are acquainted with. I have come to love broken rice (all the broken and cracked rice that has been separated from the whole grains, it has a wonderful texture). Other types routinely carried in Asian groceries include high gluten, sushi, long grain, short grain, and jasmine.

MISCELLANY

CANNED ICED COFFEE – varieties and flavors beyond even those of the average coffee shop. Most include milk and are sweetened with real sugar.

PRESERVED EGGS – also called "100 year eggs" or "century eggs"—but they're not really that old!—these are eggs (quail, chicken, or duck) that were packed in clay, lime, ash, salt, and rice straw until they turned dark. They have a creamy texture and smell like sulfur. Eat them alone or mixed into rice or soups.

QUAIL EGGS – they taste just like chicken (eggs), but are about a quarter of the size. Use them for cute deviled eggs, or a cute fried egg to put on top of a rice dish.

TEAS – black, white, green, jasmine, oolong, pearl jasmine, pearl green, and many more, sold loose, in bags, and instant.

TOFU – bean curd galore: soft, firm, spiced, smoked, fermented, dried, or fried.

EQUIPMENT

BAMBOO STEAMERS – an easy, healthy way to steam vegetables, not to mention wontons and buns. They also look attractive on the shelves of your kitchen.

CUTTING BOARDS – stylish bamboo cutting boards of all sorts (I like the round ones best).

MANDOLINES – perfect for slicing vegetables paper thin, or cutting them into ribbons.

RICE COOKERS – recommended for cooking rice, plus it will keep it warm for hours.

STRAINERS – all different sizes and grades, ranging from really fine to coarse.

WOKS – steel ones are best, but they do require a bit of maintenance.

WOODEN SPOONS – a huge selection of sizes and shapes, I really like the ones with a flat edge for nice sautéing without scratching pans.

NOTES ON INGREDIENTS AND PRODUCTS

_____
_____
_____
_____
_____

STORES

ASIA MARKET
corner of Olive Blvd. and Fee Fee Rd.
Creve Coeur

The only English sign on the outside of this store proclaims "Asia Market," so that's what I call it. It's the only full-service Korean market in town, so imagine the kimchee selection: There are standard varieties with cabbage and/or radish, cucumber kimchee, white kimchee (made without chilies so it's not spicy), kimchee with fresh or fermented fish, and "wrapped up" kimchee (vegetables are wrapped in cabbage leaves prior to fermentation, and are still wrapped up in the jar). And if you haven't experienced Korean cookies and candy, get ready for fun—think knock-off Pocky (chocolate-dipped Japanese cookie sticks) and mushroom-shaped cookies dipped in chocolate!

This is a must-visit adventure, full of hard to come by ingredients. Big red tubs of Korean hot pepper paste, jars of salted squid, and curried fish sausage are all just screaming for you to take them home and experiment. Hot and spicy Korean ramen is my favorite version of the instant noodle.

Along with the standard Asian market fare (noodles, sauces, tea, tofu), there is a whole aisle dedicated to fun, beautiful, and affordable dishes and cookware. This is where I bought my beloved, emerald green, Asian-style mandoline, the best tool to use for making thin and consistent slices of anything from potatoes to cucumbers. They also have sleek bamboo ladles, digital and flowery hot water kettles, and those handsome space stealers—bamboo steamers for steaming anything from tamales to ginger sesame marinated king ice fish.

Their produce selection is top notch, including bok choy, lettuce, spinach, eggplant, mushrooms, garlic, ginger, and potatoes. The best adventure to be had is in the meat selection. You'll find fish roe of all types, thinly sliced frozen beef and pork, frozen beef tongue, feet, and tripe. Don't miss the plethora of beef bones and the frozen black pork bacon (bacon from a black pig, a rare and sought after breed).

The employees don't speak a whole lot of English, but they are always warm, pleasant, and helpful nonetheless.

CHINA TOWN MARKET
8150 Olive Blvd
Olivette
314/993-4303

The clean and well-lit aisles of this store, along with the smiling faces of the people who work here, make it a warm and welcoming place to shop. There is an obvious Chinese flavor to China Town Market, but you can certainly find foodstuffs from Japan, Thailand, and Vietnam, including an exceptional sake selection. Instead of bringing a typical bottle of wine to the next dinner party, surprise everyone with some sake. It's great as an aperitif or with lighter courses, and you don't even have to warm it. Good sake is actually better served room temp or slightly chilled.

Very clean and well-organized produce displays and meat cases support your exploring and your likelihood to take new things home. There are piles of baby bok choy; long, shiny black eggplants; and bright green *gai lan* ("Chinese broccoli") all ready for your next stir fry. Try woody fresh lemongrass and knobby fingers of ginger to make a spicy green tea or pungent curry. They stock sausage like *lap chang*, lots of pork, chicken feet, and tripe. There is fresh and frozen fish (tilapia, cod, pike, catfish, perch, and carp), as well as shrimp.

Have I mentioned I'm a huge proponent of rice cookers? Seriously, there is no better way to cook rice. This is one great place to find rice cookers of every size and style. Their selection of countertop tea brewers/warmers is also enticing. These handy gadgets are perfect for having hot water on hand all winter long, or easily brewing iced tea in the summer.

Their dry bean selection is nothing to scoff at, with all types of dried red beans, mung beans, black mung beans, and soy beans. Use red beans in your next pot of chili along with kidney beans, replace your hummus's chickpeas with mung beans, or use all of them for gorgeous homegrown spouts.

EAST EAST ORIENTAL GROCERIES
8619 Olive Blvd.
Olivette
314/432-5590

East East is located on the busy strip of Olive Boulevard that boasts several other Asian markets and restaurants, a veritable Chinatown. This market skews a little towards the Korean offerings, though you can find plenty of Chinese, Japanese, and Vietnamese products too.

There are, of course, giant bottles of kimchee in a few different flavors, along with a few spicy pepper pastes, and fermented bean condiments. Add some Omega-3s to your next salad by making a ginger miso dressing with one of their many nori products (sheets, strips, ground, or flakes) and any of their seven types of miso paste. The sell *shiro* (white), *aka* (red), *awase* (mixed red and white), *koshi* (strained), *genen* (also a blend of red and white), organic, and sweet.

All the usual suspects fill the grocery aisles—soy sauce, tofu, ramen, sesame oil, curry paste, etc. There is a little bit of good looking produce (cabbage, sprouts, mushrooms, cilantro, potatoes, carrots, onions, eggplants, etc.). The freezer section is stocked with lots of thinly sliced beef, pork, and chicken products (easy stir fries!), my favorite being the thin sliced bone-in bacon—I've never seen it anywhere else.

The highlight of East East for me is the selection of adorable little balls of mochi ice cream (rice paste wrapped around ice cream in wonderful flavors like mango, green tea, pineapple, and coconut). Take some home for after dinner. Or after lunch. Or after for breakfast. Or for breakfast!

INTERNATIONAL FOODS
3905 S. Grand Blvd.
South City
314/351-9495

International Foods looks rather non-descript from the outside (it could easily be mistaken for a warehouse), but inside it's pretty much a trip to Southeast Asia. Not many of the signs are in English.

The fresh produce greets you first, suggestive of faraway places: Dark green limes, sprouts, green and ripe plantains, big bunches of mint and basil, three types of mangoes, and a glorious selection of mushrooms. All of it goes easy on the pocketbook.

Then there's the most foreign and most awesome help-yourself meat cooler! This cooler is a bank of small glass doors, each opening to a different cut of pork, beef, or chicken—all unwrapped and ready to be grabbed and stuffed into a small plastic bag. These unpackaged meats include pig ears, trotters, beef livers and tongue, tripe, intestines, and whole chickens. Don't worry, it's not only the weird stuff. They also have thinly sliced skirt steak, pork ribs, chunks of stew meat, and even chicken wings.

Just past the meat is the fresh seafood packed in ice, Asian and American standards like catfish, shrimp, tilapia, snapper, carp, and cod. The freezer is full of lots more seafood—about anything you could imagine—as well as egg rolls, steamed buns, and a bounty of vegetarian offerings.

Like most Asian markets, International Food overflows with noodle and instant noodle options, but it also has something I've never seen before—an equally amazing selection of dried spring roll wrappers. Find them in at least five different sizes, some even with black sesame seeds or dried shrimp mixed into the wrapper dough. (For a fun and crunchy snack, throw a wrapper into the microwave for a minute—it will puff and crisp right before your eyes.)

The cookware and dishes, a handsome range of bamboo steamers, woks, wooden spoons, rice cookers, and bowls of every size and color, will bring that certain *je ne sais quoi* to your kitchen *feng shui*.

Near the register on the way out, pick up some fresh Vietnamese baguettes for your own homemade *bahn mi* (a popular Vietnamese sandwich usually made of pork and marinated veggies and served on a baguette).

OLIVE FARMERS MARKET (OLIVE SUPERMARKET)
8041 Olive Blvd.
Olivette
314/997-5168

This place is the real deal. Starting with the stacks of Asian language newspapers by the front door and the rubber gloves worn by the cashiers, weirdly and wonderfully, you have been transported to Southeast Asia in St. Louis. Interesting and diverse products perch on the shelves, row after row, *lots* of things you can't find elsewhere in the city. Really. How about Filipino imports (like banana catsup and pickled green mangoes), live periwinkle, and frozen squab?

The name is a bit deceiving in that it's a supermarket and not a farmers market. On the other hand, the incredible selection of specialty produce and fresh herbs deserves recognition. Sick of paying $15 an ounce for exotic mushrooms? Come here for shiitakes, oysters, cremini, and French Horns at a reasonable price. Think minted peas and creminis over pasta, or creamy oyster mushroom and dill soup. Mmmm. Also look for mangosteens, chestnuts, and kumquats. Oh, and check out the bulk kimchee.

My favorite part of the store is what I call "The Dim Sum Section" (dim sum is basically the Chinese version of tapas—small, one- or two-bite foods served in many varieties)—a row of freezer cases full of sweet and savory buns filled with beans and pork and more delicious stuff, fish balls, shrimp balls, egg rolls, dumplings galore, shumai (open faced dumplings), and gyoza of every kind imaginable. Think how different Sunday brunch could be after a visit to this store!

After hosting a dim sum brunch your friends will rave about, move on to a new culinary challenge. How about a week's worth of meals based on every part of the pig? It's in the meat section here: skin, blood, liver, tongue, hooves, bung. These sit next to fresh chicken feet, stewing hen, squab, and skin-on wild boar. Imagine the possibilities!

If you aren't interested in meat, their tofu selection is the largest I've come across. Your stir fry or curry will be anything but boring once some stewed, spiced, smoked, fried, or dried tofu has been added. They even have tofu in thin sheets, and as threads reminiscent of noodles.

The fresh seafood selection is nothing to scoff at either. Alongside the standard fare (carp, flounder, tilapia, shrimp, blue crab, and catfish) are more esoteric neighbors like conch, geoduck, periwinkle, razor clam, yellow snail, sea cucumber, and skate wing.

The non-perishable products run the gamut usually found in Asian grocery stores—teas, soups, soy products, noodles, hot sauces, liquid seasonings, candies, cookies, canned drinks, and spices—plus a small number of Mexican groceries (why not?!). A couple of highlights from the shelves include palm sugar, a caramel sugar derived from palm trees that has a different and more mellow flavor than normal cane sugar, and soy sauces of every age and consistency. Not all soy sauce is like Kikkoman!

While I occasionally linger over the beer, wine, and liquors of Asian origin, I always check out the equipment: bamboo cutting boards, bamboo cooking utensils, flowery dishes, stainless steel cookware, and rice cookers of every size.

SEAFOOD CITY
7733 Olive Blvd.
Olivette
314/721-6688
See entry on p. 138.

NOTES ON CHINESE, KOREAN, AND SOUTHEAST ASIAN STORES

_____

_____

_____

_____

_____

_____

RECIPES

HOMEMADE RAMEN | SERVES 2

Dry ramen noodles (not the instant stuff with a flavor packet), cooked according to the directions on the package
4 c of chicken stock (see p. 135)
1 T ginger, minced
pulled meat from one chicken thigh (from when you made the stock)
2 t soy sauce
1 t sesame oil
1 t salt
10 snap peas, sliced
2 green onions, sliced
2 soft-boiled eggs (see p. 111)
chili–garlic paste, or Sriracha sauce, to taste

- Add stock and ginger to a small pot, and bring up to a simmer.
- Add chicken, noodles, soy sauce, sesame oil, and salt.
- Simmer for a few more minutes.
- Place soup in two bowls, garnish with snap peas, green onions, eggs, and chili–garlic paste to taste.

THAI RED COCONUT CURRY | SERVES 4–6

¼ yellow onion, chopped
1 inch of ginger, grated
4 cloves of garlic, minced
½ can Thai red curry paste (the 4 oz can from Maesri)
1 red bell pepper, sliced
1 yellow bell pepper, sliced
1 12–14 oz package of firm tofu, cut into cubes
1 15.5 fl oz can coconut milk
1½ c snap peas
salt to taste

- Heat oil in a large skillet. Add onion, and sweat until soft.
- Add garlic and ginger. Cook for another 2 minutes.
- Add curry paste, and stir constantly.
- Add peppers and tofu to the pan.
- Stir to get veggies and tofu coated in curry paste.
- Add coconut milk, and simmer for about 5 minutes.

- Turn off heat, and stir in snap peas and salt. (Don't be shy with the salt!)
- Serve immediately with brown rice.

PORK DUMPLINGS | MAKES 34

4 c savoy or napa cabbage, chopped finely
4 green onions, greens only, minced
3 cloves of garlic, minced or pressed
12 oz ground pork
1 inch of ginger, grated
1 T miso
1 T sesame oil
1 t chili–garlic paste

a package of dumpling skins
small bowl of water

- Mix the first eight ingredients in a bowl until well mixed.
- Lay out a dumpling skin and drop one T of the mixture into the middle of the skin.
- Using your finger, wet the complete edge of the dumpling skin.
- Fold the bottom half of the skin to meet the top, and crimp the folded edge six times to keep the dumpling tight.
- Repeat until all dumplings have been made.
- Add one T oil to a large skillet (one that has a tight-fitting lid) and heat until very hot, place dumplings in pan with the folded edge upright.
- Sear the bottoms of the dumplings until nicely browned.
- Add 2 T water to the pan quickly, and quickly cover with lid.
- Cook without disturbing for about 3 minutes, until dumplings are well steamed.
- Serve with equal parts soy sauce and rice vinegar, and a touch of chili garlic paste.

WATERMELON RADISH KIMCHEE | SERVES 8–10

The countertop fermentation process in this recipe is perfectly safe. Many even argue that it makes the kimchee more nutritious. This kimchee will be spicy, sour, and crisp—pretty much a perfect condiment. Don't stop at the watermelon radish, try this recipe with other types of radishes, carrots, and/or turnips. Experiment with all kinds of root vegetables.

1 lb napa or savoy cabbage, cut into large uniform chunks
3 T kosher or rock sea salt
3 lbs watermelon radish, cut into medium uniform cubes
1 thumb ginger, peeled and minced
6 cloves garlic, minced
½ c hot pepper paste (use less if you want a milder product)
¼ c fish sauce
6 scallions, cut into 2-inch sections

Notes: For hot pepper paste, I like to use the Sambal Oelek brand. Any type of fish sauce will do. Both are available at most Asian or international markets, and even a few Schnucks and Dierbergs.

- Toss the cabbage in salt until well coated.
- Squeeze the cabbage a bit in your hands to begin softening it.
- Once thoroughly coated, toss with the radish.
- Leave to sit in a bowl on the counter for 30 minutes, stirring intermittently.
- While that rests, gather remaining ingredients, except scallions, and mix them in a small bowl to form a paste.
- Clean, sanitize, and prepare 4 one-quart glass jars, or 1 one-gallon glass jar.
- Liquid should have collected at the bottom of the bowl with the cabbage and radish—do not discard. Add the scallions and the mixed paste to this bowl.
- Make sure everything is well coated with the paste.
- Transfer mixture to jar(s), pressing down to remove air bubbles and force the liquid up over the veggies.
- Cover with two layers of plastic wrap, or an airtight lid, and leave in a cool, dark place for 3 to 6 days (not cooler than 55°, and not hotter than 75°).
- Press the veggies down into the liquid twice a day until done.
- Once done fermenting, stir the contents of the jar(s).
- Place them covered into the refrigerator. In a week, they'll be ready to munch on.
- The kimchee will last in your fridge for about 6 months.

MULTIETHNIC STORES

With St. Louis being a diverse city from its very beginning, always with room for new waves of immigrants, you're going to find at least some imported items or ethnic foods on the shelves of any grocer. At the average chain store, a Schnucks or a Dierbergs, you're sure to find decent Asian, Central American, and Eastern European sections. That said, there are only two truly multiethnic grocers in St. Louis that I know of.

And so I conclude this food tour of St. Louis with these all-encompassing wonderlands, not-to-miss international adventures right at home. Enjoy! Thanks for taking this journey me and best wishes on your future explorations. Keep me posted on your findings.

GLOBAL INTERNATIONAL
globalfoodsmarket.com
421 N. Kirkwood Rd
Kirkwood
314/835-1112

Global is literally the cousin of Jay's (the other store in this chapter), as the two owners are cousins. Global, like Jay's, carries a wide range of foods from many countries across Europe and Asia, though it's a bit less gritty, with a bit higher prices in exchange.

Like Jay's, Global's whole front window is also stacked with a smorgasbord of rice varieties, in weights and bag sizes we usually associate with pet food. Unlike at Jay's, the aisles at Global are clearly marked by country, which—guess what?—makes it rather easy to find what you are looking for.

The produce here is fantastic, not only in quality, but also in selection. There are the staples, of course, but also durian, opo gourd, Chinese broccoli, eggplant, limes, avocado, bean sprouts, plantains, and mountains of seasonal vegetables.

The eye-popping dairy section takes up most of the back wall with milk-based products from just about any country you can imagine, from Bulgarian feta to cultured French butter. You've noticed that I've championed meat sections throughout this book, but Global's diversity of meat is unrivaled in St. Louis. They carry halal and kosher meat, sausages, pork and beef of all cuts, chicken, and even organ meats.

Next up: the beverage bounty. Their coffee and tea choices are super, with special Christmas and Kosher imports for the holidays. Global also stocks beer and wine from all over the world.

I cannot recommend Global enough. Go, have yourself a good browse, and tell me it didn't just make your day or week, or even change grocery shopping for the rest of your life.

JAY'S INTERNATIONAL
3172 S. Grand Blvd.
South City
314/772-2552

Located in the middle of the busy South Grand business district, Jay's International is a food paradise. When I first discovered Jay's, I used to wander up and down the aisles looking at every strange piece of produce, every label printed in a foreign language. The neighborhood surrounding this store is populated with Vietnamese, Latinos, and Bosnians, but the multiethnic products available at Jay's are certainly not limited to items from their home countries. You can also find food from all over Western Europe, Southeast Asia, the Middle East, and the Balkans.

Each aisle is jam-packed, almost floor to ceiling, with interesting and hard to find foods, including preserves, teas, cookies, pickled everything, lots of condiments (many mustards and vinegars), flours of every sort, a wide variety of grains and meals, and heat-and-serve international entrees.

When you first walk in, you are greeted by huge stacks of 25-pound sacks of rice, followed by a wall of instant noodles. In the open refrigeration you can find a variety of eggs, tofu, and organ meats.

The produce aisle is ever changing, but is usually stocked with perfectly ripe avocados, green and brown plantains, crunchy mung bean sprouts, bright green limes, giant heads of garlic, long purple Japanese eggplants, piles of jalapeños, about six types of mushrooms, and waxed yucca, just to name a few.

Like other categories here, the spice selection is vast and affordable. Consider, for example, a giant container of ground turmeric. You'll have some for potatoes and curry, and lots more for dyeing clothes and Easter eggs. Almost an entire aisle is dedicated to the largest selection of hot sauces in the city, originating everywhere from Mexico to Japan. The cheese selection happens to not be huge, but the few things they do have are priced very right—especially the feta (this could justifiably be your go-to place from now on for feta). And for the tangy labna, a Middle Eastern yogurt cheese (see p. 179).

In the freezers are tons of ready-to-cook items, such as pot stickers, fish balls (steamed balls made of seafood, vegetables, seasonings, and rice flour), meat balls, pastries, samosas, coconut ice, wontons, and steamed buns, ready for convenience or to perk up a weekday meal. Jay's meat and fish counter holds whole fish and freshly butchered beef and pork.

My favorite parts of Jay's are the bulk nuts (raw and roasted) and green coffee, the vast curry selection (from Thailand, India, Sri Lanka, China, Japan, and Vietnam), the interesting canned drinks, the fancy oils, and the mustard section.

Jay's is one of the most diverse and affordable stores in town—a must-visit, sooner rather than later!

NOTES ON MULTIETHNIC STORES

_____

_____

_____

_____

_____

_____

ACKNOWLEDGMENTS

Thanks to: Peet for driving me around; Dad for also driving me around; Mom for correcting my grammar; Rachel for being ever so supportive; Vera and Lev for keeping me inspired; Michael, Becky, and Josh for the phone calls; Erica, Chris, Sadie, and Trevor for welcoming me in and creating a lovely work environment; Halley for being excited about ingredients and for the photography work; Neil and Brea for shooting on such a tight schedule; Robert Strasser for not knowing anything about food, but still proof-reading; Mikey for the reading and listening; BJW for reading and reading and reading; Rebecca for all the rides; Jimmy Isenberg for being more nerdy about food than me; Carol for pouring hours into proof-reading; Rose for making me laugh when I felt like crying; Jim Voss for being a continued fountain of knowledge and inspiration; my coworkers, bosses, and employees at Local Harvest for all the small reminders that hard work is worth it; Sharon Woodhouse for being eternally patient and extremely supportive; Benjamin Pierce for the beautiful design; every talented chef I worked with, and who put up with my youth and ignorance; everyone who supported our Kickstarter campaign and came to our events; Joe Stein, Tina, Chris Baricevic and the South City Three for a place to stay; Ruth and all the ladies at Kitchen Conservatory for always giving me a place to come home to; and Hannah and Edward. A million extra thanks to Ruth Sparrow for last-minute research.

I never could have done this without the continuing support of every lovely person that has cheered me on, listened to me when it was hard, or celebrated when things were moving forward, including all those listed above and: Jake Jones, Dana, Hillary, Sarah Trone, The Mud House, Dan Johanning, Mike Murphy, Amanda Doyle, David and Darcie, Nick and Carol, my co-author Matt Sorrell, Adam, Michelle, Lena, Pat and Maddie, The Fortune Teller Bar, Erin Wiles, JJ Lane, Chris and Jeff, Zeng, Gary, and a million others that I can't list here because there are too many of you. And last but not least, the one person that reminds me that it's really not that bad, Ryan—I couldn't have fathomed finishing this project without your words of wisdom and supportive smile.

— *Clara Moore*

Thanks to my wife, Beth, for her unwavering support for all of my creative endeavors, and to: my mom and dad, C.W. and Carolyn Sorrell; the amazing staffs at Ladue News, FEAST Magazine, ALIVE Magazine, and Sauce Magazine for giving me a venue; and the talented men and women of the St. Louis chapter of the United States Bartenders Guild for encouraging and supporting all of my libation aspirations.

— *Matt Sorrell*

PHOTO CREDITS

INDEX: STORES, FARMERS MARKETS, AND ORGANIZATIONS

INDEX: EQUIPMENT, DISHES, AND SUPPLIES

INDEX: RECIPES

INDEX: INGREDIENTS, FOOD, AND DRINK

ABOUT THE AUTHORS

 Born and raised in St. Louis and the industry, chef, writer, teacher, and food advocate **CLARA MOORE** has worked at a wide variety of restaurants since the age of fifteen—from a 24-hour diner to haute cuisine. She started her diverse career in food and cooking working at Duff's as a busser at sixteen, eventually moving up to sous chef. At Duff's she learned culinary basics under the guidance of the talented Jim Voss, who imparted the value of using seasonal and local produce. She went on to attend culinary school at Baltimore International College and learn Mexican cooking in Guanajuato, Mexio.

In St. Louis she has worked at Trattoria Marcella and Mangia Italiano. She helped open Local Harvest Café & Catering in 2008, where she was the executive chef for almost five years. Finding food to be an important political, domestic, and public issue, she enjoyed the opportunity there to blend her passion with her values by supporting local farmers, serving seasonal foods, and creating a sustainable food community.

Clara was a contestant in Season One of Bravo's *Around the World in 80 Plates*. She thinks traditional cuisines are the most interesting and looks forward to travelling the world and eating street foods everywhere she lands.

Clara currently splits her time and culinary adventures between St. Louis and Seattle-Tacoma. She is working on the next *Shop Like a Chef* books for Tacoma and Baltimore. When in St. Louis, she is often teaching classes at Kitchen Conservatory.

Website: achefsguide.wordpress.com | Twitter: @ClaraMoore314

MATT SORRELL is a freelance writer based in St. Louis whose work has appeared in a range of local and national publications, including *USA Today, Sauce, DRAFT Magazine, ALIVE Magazine*, and *FEAST Magazine*. He writes a weekly column on local food and restaurant news, "Spicy Bits," for *Ladue News*.

Through his professional focus on food and drink he discovered a love of cocktails. His wife, Beth, followed suit, and her background as a clinical laboratory scientist soon led to an interest in the chemistry of mixing drinks. They decided to share their passion for fine libations by starting Cocktails Are Go!, a business specializing in libation education, small in-home cocktail tastings, parties, and related events.

Matt also tends bar at Salt in the Central West End. Matt and Beth live in Richmond Heights with their menagerie of cats and dogs.

Website: cocktailsarego.com | Twitter: @CockTailsAreGo

MORE

Shoplikeachef.com | www.facebook.com/ShopLikeaChef

Twitter: @ShopLikeaChef | pinterest.com/shoplikeachef

book updates, recipes, tips, author event information, and other bonuses